To Ann Hansen,
Many thanks for you[r]
wonderful help — keep up
the fight! Best wishes.
Mike Jacobson

THE BOOZE MERCHANTS
The Inebriating of America

BY MICHAEL JACOBSON,
ROBERT ATKINS
AND GEORGE HACKER

CSPI Books — Washington, D.C.

A publication of
Center for Science in the Public Interest
1501 16th St. NW, Washington, DC 20036

ISBN 0-89329-099-8
Printed in the U.S.A.
Second printing, 1984

ACKNOWLEDGEMENTS

The Booze Merchants reflects the work of many hands and minds. Steve Masley, a student at the University of Michigan, served as a hunter and gatherer of information about alcohol problems and alcohol marketing. His findings were so impressive that we decided to involve the Center further in this important public policy area.

To become immersed in the field, we asked for assistance from many people who had years of experience working on alcohol, communications, and advertising issues. Among these people were Nicholas Johnson, William Hathaway, John Pinney, Diana Tabler, Andrew Schwartzman, Michael Pertschuk, Ernest Noble, John R. DeLuca, several alcohol industry officials, and James Mosher. Jim Mosher aided us doubly by commenting on an early draft of the book.

CSPI attorney Bruce Silverglade helped analyze some of the regulatory issues, and intern Marguerite Evans scoured the libraries for relevant papers. Jim Gollin, typist *extraordinaire,* prepared the manuscript for typesetting. Greg Moyer designed the book and shepherded the manuscript and artwork through the production process, taking care of all the little details that the authors had so studiously ignored. Finally, we want to thank Burt Jackson for videotaping a battery of over-the-air alcohol ads, Nancy Drapeau for assisting with the startup of CSPI's alcohol policy project, and Ellen Suthers for compiling the index. To all these, and unnamed others, many thanks!

—Center for Science in the Public Interest

CONTENTS

CONTENTS

FOREWORD

By Nicholas Johnson

Nicholas Johnson, *a Federal Communications Commissioner from 1966–1973, currently lectures, writes and teaches from Iowa City, Iowa, about the impact of the new telecommunications on our society. He has testified before Congress and written of the impact of television on alcohol abuse.*

Massive increases in political contributions from the alcoholic beverage industry, and suppression of this report, may just be the only way to deal with it.

You can dismiss this book only if you haven't read it. It is inconceivable to me that any independent and fair-minded elected official, opinion leader, parent or citizen can read through the evidence these authors have gathered without crying out for reform.

This book does not call for a prohibition on the sale of alcohol. It studies, and speaks, of the irresponsible advertising behavior of the alcohol industry in purposely pushing its product to alcoholics, young people, and new users. It documents the industry's duplicity and hypocrisy in trying to represent the contrary to Congress.

Although neither this book, nor I, would urge the prohibition of alcohol sales, it is important to review attentively and seriously (dare one say "soberly"?) alcohol's consequences for all of us – alcoholics, moderate drinkers, and teetotalers alike.

Some liquor executives' advertising techniques would be subject to question if all they were distilling was water. But that is not the case. The alcohol industry's marketing constitutes an ethical and legal outrage precisely because of the nature and consequences of the drug it is marketing. To make light of those consequences is as cruel as it is deceptive.

The Consumers Union Report of 1972, *Licit and Illicit Drugs*, reviewed the case in a chapter entitled, "Should Alcohol be Prohibited?" Alcohol is, by any and all measures, the nation's number one hard drug.

• It involves the greatest number of users and addicts – perhaps 10 million alcoholics, and 30 million more affected co-workers and family members.

• The negative economic impact from alcohol is about $100 billion a year.

• It causes more serious and permanent destruction of the minds and bodies of its users than other drugs.

• It creates the biggest law enforcement problems – involving some 55 percent of all arrests.

• It is involved in at least half of all homocides; some experts believe it is "a necessary and precipitating element for violence."

• It is a major factor in "battered child syndrome" and battered wives.

• Suicides are linked to alcohol.

• One-half (to three-fourths) of auto accidents, including the 50,000 deaths a year, involve alcohol.

• Alcohol use and abuse is often linked to subsequent addiction to other drugs.

• It is the drug of choice for most grade school and high school students.

After reviewing this evidence, Consumers Union concluded:

> From the humanitarian as well as the societal point of view for the benefit of drinkers and potential drinkers as well as teetotalers, for the benefit of ex-heroin addicts and users of other drugs, and especially for the benefit of young people, alcohol should be promptly prohibited—except for one consideration.

That "one consideration"? "Purely pragmatic: prohibition doesn't work."

Prohibition may not work, but advertising does.

During this past decade, alcohol advertising jumped over 200 percent and is now over $1 billion annually. Sales have followed. Per capita consumption of wine, for example, is up over 65 percent. (Obviously, if the teetotalers aren't drinking, the increases are even greater for those who are.)

On the average, every man, woman and child in America over the age of 14 is now consuming, per year, 320 12-ounce cans of beer, 12 fifths of wine and ten quarts of hard liquor.

The advertising and promotion of alcoholic products in *any* media to *any* consumers at *any* time raise problems. Advertising on radio and television raises a special set of issues.

Those industries are licensed to serve "the public interest." That standard must apply not only to their programming, but also their commercials—often comprising a third or a fourth of the broadcast hour.

Thus, one must, legally, at least ask the question, "How is the 'public interest' affirmatively served by the advertising of alcohol?" How are we better off because of it? What national need is there to increase the sale of these products?

The law is clear that the "public interest" is to be paramount over the broadcasting industry's profits. But, in this instance, it is not even clear that its profits would suffer. (Broadcasting profits improved after the ban on cigarette commercials.) Other advertisers are standing in line with a multitude of less harmful products.

What broadcasters are doing, therefore, is in effect giving a preferred position to alcohol advertising. The evidence as to the adverse consequences of alcohol sales is so overpowering as to throw into serious legal question the FCC's permitting the advertising of such products at all under the "public interest" standard.

But the alcohol industry argues that their advertising isn't designed to, and doesn't, increase sales. "What?" I hear you exclaim. "Everybody knows that advertising increases sales." You may know that advertising increases sales, and I may know that advertising increases sales. But alcohol industry executives and their spokespersons have, with considerable training and practice, developed the capacity to publicly argue the contrary without so much as an embarrassed grin.

And so it is that health advocates and social scientists must be excused, once again, for going to the effort of meticulously proving and reporting what "everybody knows."

As shocking as you may find this statement, the fact is that U.S. public policy on alcohol advertising is today based on the industry's sworn, but unproven, assertion that all they are trying to buy with their $1 billion is a shift in brand loyalty.

They have repeated it so often that politicians and regulators have come to believe and act upon it.

Drawing upon statements and publications of alcohol executives themselves, *The Booze Merchants* documents how the alcohol industry has been playing fast and loose with the truth. Its spokespeople have misrepresented the purposes of the industry's advertising and its effects.

"Marketing" is, today, a sophisticated specialty of study. Gone are the days of Willy Loman (the salesman in *Death of a*

Salesman) with his "smile and a shoeshine." Business schools are turning out graduate students who are adept at using computers to solve sales problems. "Psychographics" are designed to aim ad campaigns at the psychological cravings of targeted subsets of potential customers.

Here's one example of how advertisers are out to get you:

A firm called Behavior Scan uses modern telecommunications technologies to give advertisers overnight results on the effectiveness of new TV commercials.

"Bar code" readers (grocery counter magic that reads the little line codes marked on each product) are provided all grocery and drug stores in selected communities. Shoppers who participate in the test are given plastic identification cards. Their every purchase is recorded on a computer.

Un-used cable television channels are used to "switch" test ads into the commercial breaks of conventional TV programs, unknown to the audience. A home computer records which programs, and commercials, the test consumers view. A computer in Chicago calls each of the home computers at night, while the people sleep.

By matching what viewers watch with what they buy, Behavior Scan can tell advertisers which commercials produce the greatest sales.

Not only are the techniques available, but so are the strategies. The popular management consultant Peter Drucker often argued that one of business' greatest errors was misallocation of resources. He noted that 90 percent of the energy often goes to produce 10 percent of the sales, and urged a reversal of those figures.

The alcohol industry is following Drucker's suggestions.

Alcoholics and problem drinkers account for some 50 to 70 percent of sales. Common sense, as well as a sophisticated marketing strategy, suggests that this "profit center" should be the target of advertising—so long as alcohol advertising and promotion is considered legal.

Although marketing executives profess the contrary, only they will be shocked by the rather obvious finding that the industry is—in the same way and for the same reasons as the heroin dealer—pushing drugs to addicts.

Of course alcoholics are not the only targeted audience. The late Robert Kennedy used to campaign in high schools—even though he knew the kids couldn't vote. Alcoholic beverage companies advertise and promote to the same youngsters (often legally prohibited from drinking)—for the same reason.

As this report quotes one marketing executive as saying:

> Let's not forget that getting a [college] freshman to choose a certain brand of beer may mean that he will maintain his brand loyalty for the next twenty to thirty-five years. If he turns out to be a big drinker, the beer company has bought itself an annuity.

Yes, the industry is trying to increase sales in every possible market—heavy drinkers, light drinkers, young people, women. And it is succeeding. Advertising pays. Sales are up. Its markets are expanding.

We are encouraged to increase the occasions and length of time when we drink, the quantities of alcohol we consume each time, the variety of alcoholic beverages we drink, the age at which it is permissible to drink.

Industry trade association standards of ethical alcohol advertising are openly and flagrantly breached, notwithstanding industry protestations to the contrary. And that hypocrisy is repeatedly documented throughout the book.

Why is this occurring? What can be done about it?

Shareholders cannot expect executives to violate the law. They can expect management to maximize profit within the law. Our laws and regulations create a network of rewards and punishments, incentives and disincentives, within which corporate behavior is shaped.

So long as our lawmakers continue to permit any alcohol advertising at all, they must share responsibility for corporate policies designed to increase sales, increase the number of alcoholics and the consumption of each, and encourage the addiction of our children. Those are simply the natural and predictable consequences of current policies.

The authors of the *The Booze Merchants* offer quite reasonable and balanced suggestions for reform. In fact, my only disagreement is a fear that they have compromised too much. What I think their book offers us is the documentation of our common sense: the only solution is a total, legally enforced ban on the advertising or promotion of alcoholic products of any kind to any group of customers at any time.

It is naive to believe that any precisely honed standards for regulating "abuses" can withstand evasion by ingenious advertising agency executives and promotion schemes.

Whatever guilt the more responsible alcohol executives may carry inside them, it is psychologically unrealistic (and even unfair) to hope that any amount of "tsk, tsk" appeals to conscience, or hortatory language from governments or trade associations can possibly alter their profit-maximizing behavior without a change in the law.

Such changes are inevitable once a civilized society understands the evidence and message of this book. They have occurred in such places as Ecuador, Finland, India, New Zealand, Norway, Switzerland and Venezuela. Let us hope *The Booze Merchants* is promptly and widely read and acted upon in the United States as well.

—April, 1983.

1.

*"Getting back to the idea that
what advertising can accomplish
is quite limited, advertisers don't
even try to reach non-drinkers."*

Sam Chilcote
Former president of DISCUS
Distilled Spirits Council of the U.S.

America's Number One Drug Problem

"Alcohol." The familiar liquid that this seven-letter word represents is responsible for one of the most expensive and serious group of public health problems in the United States today. The economic costs related to alcohol abuse far exceed those due to virtually every other disease. Alcohol problems touch every American, drinker or not. And the alcoholic beverage industry, through its marketing activities, affects practically everyone old enough to watch television or listen to the radio.

In 1975, the National Institute on Alcohol Abuse and Alcoholism (NIAAA) reported that alcohol-related health costs amounted to nearly $43 billion.[1] Those costs included lost productivity, health care, automobile accidents, fire damage, social responses like treatment programs and highway safety

It's Miller Time: The cabbie goes off duty and into the local tavern for some brew. The question is, will he be able to drive home?

measures, violent crime, and criminal justice. The NIAAA also estimated in 1975 that 205,000 deaths, 11 percent of the year's total, were alcohol related.[2] A subsequent study by the National Academy of Sciences criticized the NIAAA study as being methodologically limited and estimated alcohol-related costs to be $60 billion. In March, 1983, the Congressional office of Technology Assessment estimated that "the economic cost of alcoholism and alcohol abuse . . . may be as high as $120 billion annually."[2A]

The bare statistics are mind-boggling, but do not even begin to capture the gruesome human effects of alcohol abuse and alcoholism. A person whose life is controlled by the bottle is often unable to keep a job and support a family. A male alcoholic may respond to his wife's expression of concern by beating her. A female alcoholic may ignore the needs of her children. A young alcoholic still in school, may lose interest in his or her studies and never achieve academic or business success. A person whose thought pattern is warped by alcohol is often emboldened to commit a crime that he or she never would have done when sober.

Alcoholics seem to lose interest in family, friends, and life itself and become a drain on, rather than contributors to, socie-

Table 1-1: Alcoholic Beverage Industry's 1982 Ad Spending*
($ million)

Medium	Wine	Distilled Spirits	Beer	Total	% Change From 1970
Radio	$ 17.1	—	$117.0	$134.1	+240%
Television	143.6	—	366.9	510.5	+441
Magazine	12.5	$223.3	21.6	257.4	+160
Outdoor	1.1	75.8	11.4	88.3	+152
Newspaper	13.2	76.5	16.5	106.2	+ 62
Supplements	1.6	10.3	0.3	12.2	+510
Total	$189.1	$385.9	$533.7	$1,108.7	+231%

Source: **Advertising Age**, July 15, 1983

*Substantial marketing expenses other than measured media advertising are not included in these figures.

Table 1-2: Per Capita Consumption of Alcoholic Beverages
(gallons)

	1970	1975	1980	Percent Change 1970–80
Beer	18.5	21.3	24.3	+31%
Spirits	1.82	1.97	1.98	+ 9.3
Wine	1.26	1.68	2.08	+65
Total	21.58	24.95	28.36	+31.5

Source: **The Brewers Almanac 1981,** The U.S. Brewers Association

Table 1-3: Percent Change in Production: Actual and Predicted

	1960–1980	1970–1980	1980–1990
Wine	192.0%	78.3%	126.1%
Spirits	85.0%	17.3%	19.8%

Source: **The Impact Distilled Spirits Review,** 1981

ty. A person who is not an alcoholic, but drinks too much from time to time can be variously obnoxious, irresponsible, or dangerous—to himself or herself or to others. Anyone whose father, mother, good friend, or acquaintance drinks heavily knows all too well the devastating impact of beverages that are portrayed just like soda pop in upbeat, humorous television commercials.

Alcohol commercials, of course, are not the only ads to which we are exposed. Americans live in a veritable sea of advertising. Just as fish take their home of water for granted, most people accept advertising as just another aspect of contemporary life. Advertising, be it for mattresses or make-up, is a sophisticated art, making use of decades of accumulated knowledge and experience, playing on the consumer's most private insecurities, fears, and desires.

Advertising not only affects our purchasing decisions; it also affects our vision of society, our attitudes toward other people, and our philosophical beliefs. While these effects are of great importance, advertising deserves the greatest scrutiny when it promotes the sale of products that cause illness or death. Such

Chart 1-A

TRENDS IN APPARENT PER CAPITA ETHANOL CONSUMPTION IN U.S. GALLONS, BASED ON BEVERAGE SALES IN EACH MAJOR BEVERAGE CLASS IN THE UNITED STATES, 1944 - 1978

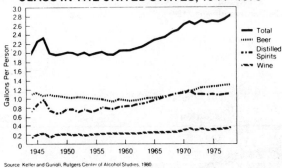

Source: Keller and Gurioli, Rutgers Center of Alcohol Studies, 1980.

has been the case for cigarettes, which kill tens of thousands of people a year – and our society has decided that it is inappropriate to advertise cigarettes on radio and television. Such could also be the case for alcoholic beverages, the use of which is related to well over 100,000 deaths a year and costs society tens of billions of dollars.

The rising toll of alcohol problems has been paralleled in the last two decades by greatly increased alcohol advertising and by increased consumption of alcohol. (See Tables 1-1, 1-2, 1-3, and Chart 1-A.) Only a very naive person would argue that the massive amounts of sophisticated and expensive marketing efforts do not tend to whitewash the dangers of alcohol by imbuing alcoholic beverages with an image of total harmlessness and by reinforcing drinking as the social norm.

Considering the problems associated with drinking, the growth in advertising and consumption is of particular interest. Between 1970 and 1978, *per capita* consumption of total alcohol increased by 15 percent. In terms of volume, the beer industry has set the pace, with a six-gallon per year (31 percent) increase in *per capita* consumption between 1970 and 1980. The wine industry has experienced almost meteoric growth, with a 65 percent increase in *per capita* consumption in that same decade. In fact, in terms of fluid volume per person, wine passed distilled spirits in 1980 for the first time ever in the U.S. Currently, the "average" U.S. resident 14 years old and above downs about 320 12-ounce cans of beer, 12.5 fifths of table wine, and 10.5 quarts of distilled spirits in a year. In 1982, alcohol consumption declined a tiny bit, presumably due to the major recession and double-digit unemployment.

Between 1970 and 1981, advertising expenditures by alcohol companies jumped 203 percent. In 1981, alcohol ad budgets surpassed $1 billion for the first time (see Appendix for details), and there is no sign of a let-up (of course, inflation has contributed its share to the hefty increases). Wine advertis-

ing on television jumped by 30 percent in the first nine months
of 1982 compared to 1981, while beer advertising increased
17 percent.[3]

Much more than just the quantity of advertising has increased, though. With the entry of experienced marketers like
Philip Morris (owner of Miller Brewing Company) and Coca-
Cola (owner of The Wine Spectrum) into the alcohol business,
more sophisticated marketing programs have been developed.
Advertisements have been behaviorally designed to appeal to
the personality of drinkers. "Psychographics" are the key to
successful ad campaigns – that is, ads which appeal to the psychology of specific target audiences. Promotion and packaging have been updated as well to include such ideas as college
campus beer representatives, dollars-off coupons, rock concerts,
the use of celebrities, partial sponsorship of the Olympics,
plastic liquor bottles, and six-packs of canned wine. Alcohol
producers, continually testing the limits dictated by social attitudes, are learning that they can market with few restrictions a psychoactive and potentially addictive drug.

The question remains whether or not this drastic increase
in the cost and quality of marketing expenditures contributes
to increased consumption. The fact is, little high-quality, independent research has been done on this topic. The most ex-
haustive work completed to date was published by researchers
Charles Atkin and Martin Block of Michigan State University
in 1981.[4] Their $100,000, 400-page study, entitled "Content
and Effect of Alcohol Beverage Advertising," was prepared for
the Bureau of Alcohol, Tobacco and Firearms, Federal Trade
Commission, Department of Transportation, and NIAAA.

Atkin and Block concluded that advertising increases consumption by at least 10 percent, prompts excessive drinking,
and influences the values and behavior of consumers, especially adolescents. Their research methodology, however, suffered
from a variety of limitations and their findings are not

definitive (the same could be said about most studies in this field). In *The Booze Merchants*, we will refer to data in the Michigan State study, but generally not to the researchers' conclusions.

The other body of research we will refer to frequently was carried out by Warren Breed and James DeFoe of the Scientific Analysis Corporation in San Francisco and Berkeley, California. Dr. Breed is the director of the Alcohol, Mass Media, and Public Education Project. Much of their work has been funded by NIAAA, as well. Breed and DeFoe are among the few independent researchers who have examined alcohol advertising in magazines and newspapers and the depiction of alcohol on television shows. The frequent reference to the Michigan State study and Breed and DeFoe's work reflects more the paucity of research in the field than the comprehensiveness of these studies.

Representatives of the alcohol industry have also sponsored research and maintain – at least in public – that any relationship between increased advertising and increased consumption is purely coincidental. Beer, wine, and spirits makers generally argue that advertising and promotion are intended solely to shift current drinkers from one brand to another.

"The major function of advertising is to obtain an increase in the market share rather than to artificially stimulate alcohol consumption," said David Pittman, chairman of the Sociology department at Washington University.[5] Pittman, who is a paid consultant to the beer and liquor industries, has written and testified that there is no link between advertising and increased consumption. Under the aegis of the Social Science Institute, Pittman and his colleagues have publicized the absence of scientific proof linking advertising and consumption.[6]

People within the industry are equally assertive about the limits of their advertising, when they go on the public record.

For instance, Kathleen Ryan of Miller Brewing Company's
Corporate Affairs office said that beer marketing is "brand
competition within an established market. It is just like one
person may want a Hershey's chocolate bar and another a
Clark Bar." When asked directly if alcohol marketing attempted to increase the market size or individual consumption,
Ryan said that the purpose of advertising is "to appeal to existing beer drinkers."[7] The industry in general denies that it
employs marketing tactics that appeal to vulnerable groups,
like heavy drinkers or young people, to increase sales and
consumption.

Sam Chilcote, then president of the Distilled Spirits Council of the United States (DISCUS), the liquor industry's trade
group, said in 1980, "Getting back to the idea that what advertising can accomplish is quite limited, advertisers don't even
try to reach non-drinkers."[8]

The Booze Merchants describes many of the ways in which
alcoholic beverages are being marketed. These range from
familiar advertising to little-known gimmicks. Still, this report
is limited, because most of the industry's plans to get Americans to drink are closely held secrets (an understandable practice, especially for this industry). Also, we have largely ex-
cluded such innovations as new forms of packaging (plastic
liquor bottles and canned wine) and new products (pre-mixed
cocktails, low-calorie beer and wine), as well as the marketing
programs directed at distributors and retailers, newspaper discount coupons, and retail liquor store ads.

Some of the important questions about alcohol marketing
that deserve careful investigation by concerned citizens and
policy makers include:

• Do marketing efforts increase overall consumption or just
cause consumers to switch from one brand to another? In other
words, is it worth even being concerned about advertising?

• Do advertisers ever appeal to non-drinkers?

• Do alcohol marketers target young people, even those below legal drinking age?

• Do advertisers target heavy drinkers, whose ranks include millions of alcoholics?

• What long-term effects do alcohol marketing programs have on public attitudes regarding alcohol and drinking?

• Have governmental agencies been effective watchdogs of alcohol marketing?

Conclusive answers to these questions will require much new research and study by independent psychological and marketing experts in the academic community. Our intent is to highlight some of the most recent, typical, and sometimes dramatic strategies in advertising, promotion, and packaging. The compilation of quotes, examples and explanations, we believe, accurately conveys the purpose of alcohol marketing efforts. But before turning to actual ads and promotional schemes, let us look briefly at the voluntary and governmental mechanisms that have been designed to regulate the marketing of alcoholic beverages.

Societies have long recognized the hazards posed by alcoholic beverages. Consequently, both government and the industries themselves have taken a few steps to monitor and regulate the advertising of the products.

To maintain an image of responsibility and discourage practices that would reflect poorly on the industry, the trade associations that represent the great majority of domestic spirits, wine, and beer makers have established advertising codes. These codes are voluntary guidelines for ethical practices, although they only apply to advertising, not the whole realm of marketing techniques. The most widely known code restrictions are the prohibition of distilled spirits ads on television or radio (this voluntary prohibition began breaking down in

Traditionally, wine ads were soft-spoken and depicted wine as part of the meal. That was before wine companies broadened their appeal to become an "everytime" beverage. Dignity is thrown out the door by the makers of "Wild Irish Rose" in this sexually suggestive ad.

1982) and the taboo on the actual drinking of alcohol in commercials (which, in early 1983, appears to be on the verge of breaking down). Some of the codes also discourage appeals to children, the use of sexuality, the exploitation of women, and the use of bad taste.

The ad codes vary in their breadth and specificity. *The Code of Good Practice* adopted in 1975 by the Distilled Spirits Council of the United States (DISCUS) is the least detailed and relies mostly on broad statements like, "All advertisements of distilled spirits shall be modest, dignified and in good taste."[9] DISCUS applies the same language to the depiction of women in ads.

The U.S. Brewers Association's *Guidelines For Beer Advertising* (1975) discourages ads that contain appeals for overindulgence, links to dangerous or criminal activities, depictions of loss of self control, even slightly lewd or obscene material, the use of young models, and the depiction of unkempt taverns.[10]

The Wine Institute's *Code of Advertising Standards* (1978) discourages certain approaches that are sometimes used by the hard liquor and beer industries. It disallows ads that suggest excessive drinking and the use of wine in conjunction with dangerous activities and driving. The *Code* discourages the kind of lifestyle ads that are the mainstay of liquor and beer advertising: "Any attempt to suggest that wine directly contributes to success or achievement is unacceptable. . . . Wine shall not be presented as being essential to personal performance, social attainment, achievement, success or wealth."[11] The use of wine for personal problem solving, social acceptance, or entertainment is also found unacceptable. The Institute also bars strategies that appeal to youth: young models, youth music, and celebrities, as well as placing ads in "youth-oriented media," are all Wine Institute no-nos.

Industry's advertising codes make little effort to extend comparable standards beyond advertising. Marketing and promotion strategies which might be used to expand the market and encourage greater consumption are not mentioned. As we will discuss, the restrictions on appeals to youth and heavy drinkers, depictions of dangerous activities, the use of sexuality, and associations with success are regularly violated in ads and in other marketing efforts. The domestic firms which do not belong to the associations, most notably the liquor producer Heublein, and foreign producers of Lambrusco wines (Riunite, Giacobazzi) and tequilas and rum (Cuervo Tequila, Cruzan Rum), are the most blatant violators. However, many domestic and foreign producers engage in marketing practices that violate the letter and spirit of these codes in an effort to expand their markets and increase consumption. .

Any enforcement of advertising guidelines by the several trade associations is done secretly, with no publicity whatsoever. Consequently, we cannot judge the trade associations' claims that they do work effectively behind the scenes. It is clear, though, judging from ads, that many companies don't pay them much heed.

Federal laws and regulations also regulate alcohol advertising. The Federal Trade Commission (FTC), which oversees all advertising, and the Bureau of Alcohol, Tobacco, and Firearms (BATF), a division of the Treasury Department, share the oversight of alcohol advertising.

The Federal Trade Commission is the government agency most experienced in regulating advertising and marketing practices. The FTC Act forbids "unfair or deceptive" marketing practices, but contains nothing specific to alcoholic beverages. From time to time the FTC has investigated specific alcoholic beverage ads. In 1976 the FTC staff asked for authority to *subpoena* information from Anheuser-Busch, Inc., the largest producer of beer (Budweiser), and Somerset Importers, Ltd., a major marketer of alcoholic beverages (Johnnie Walker), to help determine whether these firms ever engaged in unfair advertising.

The FTC staff said,

> We have received information which suggests that one company, Anheuser-Busch, may have attempted to target certain of its advertisements at a group of drinkers which appear to contain an unusually high proportion of persons who tend to be subject to alcohol abuse. . . . We believe that an attempt to sell alcoholic beverages by appeals directed to an unusually vulnerable portion of the population, a portion for whom drinking may involve major health risks, raises serious issues of unfairness under section 5 [of the Federal Trade Commission Act].

The FTC staffers also said that, in the case of Somerset Importers, they had

> found some indication that this major marketer of alcoholic beverages has also been involved in research that could aid it in targeting advertisements to problem drinkers. . . . Four advertisements have come to our attention in the past year that appeared to warrant some further inquiry. Each of these also appeared to us, at least, improperly to hold out the advertised brand as a solution for a variety of personal problems.

The FTC staff was authorized to push ahead with its investigation, but about a year later, in 1977, the staff decided it was necessary to ask for industry-wide *subpoena* authority. That request was deferred until the completion of the Atkin-Block study, because it was recognized that further research was necessary before making recommendations "in an advertising field as heavily politicized as alcoholic beverages." After the study was completed, the staff reported back to the Commission in 1981. It stated, in a memo to the Commission, "reluctance to pursue these investigations against individual companies where it appeared that the promotional practices questioned might be widespread in the industry." It recommended that the individual investigations be closed, but requested direction from the Commission on whether any further investigation should be pursued.[12]

FTC Commissioner Michael Pertschuk argued that when problems are as widespread as in the alcohol industry, an industry-wide rule is needed.[13] On September 20, 1982, however, the FTC Commissioners voted 3–1 (only Commissioner Pertschuk dissenting) to terminate the two specific investigations. The commission did not open an industry-wide inquiry. This is the strange way that alcoholic beverage advertising is handled by the nation's top advertising regulatory agency during the Reagan Administration.

The Bureau of Alcohol, Tobacco and Firearms can also crack down on unfair or deceptive advertising.[14] Whereas the FTC is concerned with advertising for all enterprises in the U.S., BATF has a much narrower focus. Its regulations are also comparatively specific. For liquor, beer, and wine ads, BATF prohibits "false," "misleading," "obscene," or "indecent" statements. More broadly, the Federal Alcohol Administration Act prohibits any statement relating to "irrelevant" matters, irrespective of falsity, which the Secretary of the Treasury finds to be likely to mislead the consumer.[15]

Judging from the prevalence of questionable ads and marketing practices, the BATF seems to be asleep at the wheel. Though a great deal of advertising appears on radio and television, the agency has no way of regularly monitoring these media. The advertising regulatory enforcement staff of one or two people is limited to thumbing through newspapers and magazines. We are unaware of any agency inquiry into effects of advertising on young children, heavy drinkers, and other segments of the population or into non-advertising marketing practices that appear aimed at the young. Based on our conversations with officials of BATF, regulation of advertising and marketing holds a rather low priority. We shall not speculate why at this point. Instead, let's see what the marketing executives – not the pacifying press releases of the P.R. flaks – have to say about the function of advertising and promotional efforts by the alcoholic beverage industry.

2.

*"We look forward to the 80s as
a period of excitement and growth
marked by one word: marketing."*

— *Impact*/ Market Review and Forecast (1980)

Inside the Industry

After bedeviling society for centuries, alcoholic beverages
have gained their share of critics. The strongest repudiation
of alcohol in modern times was surely Prohibition, which lasted
from 1920 to 1933. Then, reformers didn't mince words or talk
compromise. They said, "Let's just get rid of alcohol." While
their victory was a success in terms of the public's health – alcohol-related diseases declined dramatically in that era – it
flopped as social policy. Alcoholic beverages are back, and back
for good.

Since Prohibition, most people concerned about problems
caused by alcohol have grown to accept the presence of the products. But eager to reduce alcohol's harm to society in some way,
they have offered reforms that would make Prohibitionists

blanch. These people, whose ranks include public health officials, legislators, professors, and many other concerned citizens, frequently charge that alcoholic beverage producers aim a good portion of their marketing dollar at youths, alcoholics, non-drinkers, and certain other segments of the population. These critics – snidely dubbed "neo-Prohibitionists" by some in the industry – contend that the marketers target people most easily harmed by alcohol and people who are most vulnerable to advertising messages. They further contend that industry tries to lure new drinkers into the fold and to increase total consumption as much as possible. In this section, we shall ignore the critics. Instead we will put our ear to the closed doors of the alcoholic beverage companies and listen in on corporate officials themselves.

The marketing of products and commercial growth are not undesirable *per se.* They are part and parcel of most American business strategies. Ad executive Charles Sharp of Charles Sharp Associates, Los Angeles, said, "I am confident that any private enterprise, whether the automobile business or the liquor business, is trying to keep their business by expanding their market."[16]

Appealing to a specific group of people in order to sell more sofas or shoes is not irresponsible – increased buying of furniture or shoes is not hazardous to one's health. On the other hand, appealing to heavy drinkers to consume more liquor could have fatal consequences to the drinkers or others. Using sophisticated psychological strategies to coax light drinkers or non-drinkers, like teenagers or women, to imbibe also poses great potential dangers. Growth in the furniture business means that more people buy more tables and chairs; growth in the alcoholic beverage business unfortunately means more alcohol abuse and alcoholism. In fact, the potential for serious physical or social harm is the very reason why the alcohol industry publicly disclaims any effort to increase consumption, a remarkable and barely believable assertion by business people.

Occasional candid statements by alcohol executives, business analysts, and trade journalists provide an insider's view of the industry's intentions. These statements illustrate the assumptions that underlie marketing decisions. The dominant theme throughout is the equation of business growth with greater consumption.

The leader in the beer market, Anheuser-Busch (A-B), is proud of and frank about its confirmed success in the wake of a marketing attack waged by Miller Brewing Co., the number two brewer. The president of A-B's beer division, Dennis Long, now suggests that there is more growth potential beyond the existing market: "If you segment this country geographically, demographically and by competitors, it gives you great confidence that there is still considerable room for us to grow."[17] Since Anheuser-Busch appears to have won the battle for the "King of Beers" spot, it has been working to take advantage of that room. It has dramatically increased its capital spending program to increase plant capacity by 27 percent within five years.[17] *The New York Times* says this is, "To meet the demand it hoped to generate...."[18]

Rather than meeting the demand of the current market, as the industry generally claims it does, A-B plans to generate more demand through marketing. More demand means more consumption. Marketing vice president for Anheuser-Busch, Michael Roarty, explains how this has happened: "The creative concept [advertising] combined with our strong emphasis on sports, on tv and radio in our grassroots approach to local sports have been responsible for the continued growth at Budweiser."[19]

Participants in the booming wine business are even more candid about the marketing future of wine. The euphoria over the 65 percent increase in *per capita* consumption in the last decade has left wine analysts and producers scheming for more. The widely read in-trade *Wine Marketing Handbook* suggested in 1979 that "the wine industry must in addition to cultivating a higher frequency rate *in today's prime wine markets—promote greater wine usage* in areas of the nation which are not yet wine-conscious."[20] (emphasis added) Translated, the *Handbook* suggests that the wine industry encourage current drinkers to drink more and expand the market by creating new drinkers.

Wine and spirits analyst and consultant Marvin Shanken (publisher of the alcohol trade journals *Impact* and *Market Watch*) says that the wine industry has the potential to expand its "user base" by 75 percent and that current drinkers can be encouraged to consume more. At a business conference recently, Shanken said, "The mind boggles at the heights wine consumption could reach if light drinkers could be nudged up to medium and *medium up to heavy.* Coke and Pepsi watch out!"[21] (emphasis added) Shanken is not only suggesting that wine should compete with soda, but he is proposing that marketers help create heavy wine drinkers. Substituting alcoholic beverages for soda and other non-alcoholic beverages is, in fact, one way marketers hope to increase consumption. Speaking of soda and tea, *The Wine Handbook* states, "Each of these

Wine advertising and wine sales have grown greatly in recent years, due in part to a conscious effort on industry's part to boost U.S. consumption to Old World levels. This ebullient Italian reinforces the European wine mystique.

beverages may be considered to be in direct competition with table wines, the industry's chief hope for bringing about an improved frequency rate."[22]

Wine industry executives and their advertising agents are equally enthusiastic about the growth of wine. Bill Tenebrusso, the ad agent who manages Coca-Cola's Wine Spectrum (Taylor and Great Western Wines) account at Kenyon & Eckhardt, says, "I think the wine business is going to try to broaden its consumer base. We'd like to see *per capita* consumption increase 2.5 gallons."[23]

Peter Sealey, vice president for the *Wine Spectrum*, told *Business Week* magazine, "We should be able to double consumption *per capita* to four gallons by 1990."[24] Sealey was not predicting a natural occurrence, but conveying the projected impact of Coke's marketing efforts to actively increase consumption. *Business Week* added, "Coke and its competitors are seeking to expand the market still more through product innovation, new types of packaging, varied sales outlets, and heavy advertising." Obviously, *Business Week* has not been persuaded by industry's P.R. flaks that there is no relationship between marketing and increased consumption.

Margaret Stern, a vice-president of the Wine Spectrum, has predicted the future of the wine industry, a future that is to a great extent dictated by the marketing plans of her company. She wrote in the 100th-anniversary issue of *Beverage World* magazine that:

> By 1992, wine will be more widely distributed; more st. s appear to be electing for the sale of wine in food stores. Currently, only about half the restaurants in the U.S. licensed to sell alcoholic beverages sell wine. That percentage will near 100 percent in the next ten years, and restaurants where alcohol is not now served will add wine service. Fast food restaurants will begin selling wine and more carry-out establishments will add wine for their patrons.[23]

As one way to make wine more convenient for restaurants

to serve, Wine Spectrum markets 18-liter bag-in-box containers.

Criticizing one branch of the wine business, *Impact*'s Marvin Shanken also recognized the advertising-consumption relationship: "The industry would love to attract new consumers through light wines, but that's a function of advertising. The theory of marketing is to bring new customers to the marketplace. . . . "[25]

The distilled spirits industry is in a period of self-examination because of its recent lackluster performance. The liquor industry suffered its worst year in a decade in 1980 with shipments of spirits down 3.7 percent,[26] and 1982 was little better, with a two percent decline.[27] In addition, the nature of the industry itself has changed as sales of traditional "brown goods" (whiskey, scotch, bourbon) declined in favor of "white goods" (gin, vodka, rum and tequila). In 1960, brown liquor held 74 percent of the market and white had only 19 percent. By 1975, the shares changed to 54 percent and 35 percent and in 1980, 45 percent and 39.5 percent. Many industry observers predict that white goods will pass brown in the 1980s.[28]

Although these changes were met by drastic slowing of advertising spending in 1980, distillers increased their ad budgets eight percent in 1981. The 1980 *Impact—Market Review and Forecast* said, "We look forward to the 80s as a period of excitement and growth marked by one key word: marketing."[29] Responding to declines in the sales of brown goods and foreseeing the current slump, the president of Hiram Walker, Roy W. Stevens, said in 1977, "We've got to persuade more people to drink whiskey."[20] Commenting on new marketing plans to increase whiskey consumption, *Fortune* magazine made contrasts to the old marketing thinking: "Looking back on that era, the liquor marketing strategies of those decades now seem simple—a matter mainly of pitting brand against brand within clearly defined categories like blended whiskeys, bourbon or scotch."[30] *Fortune* implies that today liquor marketers are attempting to expand the whole market rather than just selling particular labels.

While academics debated whether advertising actually increases consumption of alcohol, *Technology Illustrated* magazine ran a two-page ad that described succinctly what it felt ads in that magazine could do for liquor companies. The bold headline read, "How to accelerate the flow of America's essential liquids."[31]

Vincent Machi, chairman of the Distilled Spirits Council of the United States, made a revealing remark at the Council's Ninth Annual Conference in early 1982. Machi proudly recalled the liquor industry's 1981 triumphs, including, among others, the defeat of ingredient labeling and excise tax increases. He also was gratified that "the military withdrew their plan to cut consumption by making the 1.75 liter a two-punch item on the ration card for soldiers in Europe."[32] Consumption is clearly the obsession of the liquor business when even cutting the alcohol intake of American soldiers is perceived as a threat to profits.

Finally, there is general agreement in business circles that advertising affects consumption beyond particular brands and can promote an entire category or market. That is, advertising for one brand boosts all brands. Ad executive Charles Sharp refers to advertising as a tool "which serves more like a shotgun than a rifle."[16] Its impact hits multiple targets, not just one. A former president of the American Tobacco Company, George Washington Hill, said about advertising, "You don't benefit yourself most, I mean altogether. Of course you benefit yourself more than the other fellow if you do a good job, but you help the whole industry if you do a good job."[33] Therefore, by default, advertising can have a much broader effect than just brand preference. For instance, in a special issue on liquor marketing, *Advertising Age* suggested, "Thus advertising for Smirnoff vodka helps Smirnoff sales, but it also gives a boost to vodka in general."[28] In the furniture business such a marketing phenomenon would not harm the public's health or welfare. In the alcoholic beverage business, however, the "shot gun effect" contradicts the industry's public position by promoting liquor in general, possibly leading to heavier drinking.

We have heard some industry executives describe their visions of greater alcohol consumption in the U.S. Let us now examine some of the measures they have implemented to achieve their goal.

PART 1: INCREASING CONSUMPTION AND EXPANDING THE MARKET

The alcohol industry's program to increase consumption and expand the market is varied in terms of targets and techniques. The primary attention of marketers appears focused on heavy drinkers, young people, and special categories such as blacks, women, and people who do not like the taste of alcohol. The marketing strategies for capturing these consumers include not only ad design and placement, but new products for new markets, promotional activities such as sports and music events, and increased retail availability such as wine in fast food restaurants. In this section we will focus on advertising and promotional programs. Closer analyses of ad placement, promotional activities, and ad content will be presented later.

"Michelob after work
makes you glad there's a rush ho...

MICHELOB

BEER

Put a little
weekend
in your wee...

3.

"If all 105 million drinkers of legal age consumed the official maximum "moderate" amount of alcohol, the industry would suffer 'a whopping 40 percent decrease in the sale of beer, wine, and distilled spirits, based on 1981 sales figures'."

Robert Hammond
Director, Alcohol Research Information Service

Targeting the Heavy Drinker

Heavy drinkers make up one of the two top target groups for alcohol marketing. Not only are heavy drinkers—which include problem drinkers and alcoholics—vulnerable to advertising because of their existing or developing psychological commitment and physiological addiction to booze, but they consume between 50 and 70 percent of all alcoholic beverages. Every industry will court most assiduously its most frequent and biggest customers. (Of course, we do not believe that alcoholics would quickly put down their bottle were advertising totally abolished; advertising is just one of many factors that influence drinking habits.)

The exact definition and number of heavy drinkers varies from source to source. The National Institute on Alcohol Abuse and Alcoholism defines heavy drinkers as those consuming two or more drinks a day; they make up 11 percent of the adult population. The heavy drinker consumes an average of 1.0 or more ounces of ethanol a day (about 2 drinks), compared to 0.22–0.99 ounces for moderate drinkers and 0.1–0.21 for light drinkers.[34] Some marketers estimate that heavy drinkers constitute up to 20 percent of the adult population. Whatever the exact figure, it is clear that heavy drinkers are a minority group that consumes the majority of alcohol.

Despite the alcoholic beverage industry's occasional sanctimonious pleas for people to drink in moderation, the industry would suffer a severe shrinkage if everyone obeyed the moderation message. Alcohol critic Robert Hammond, director of Alcohol Research Information Service, has estimated that if all 105 million drinkers of legal age consumed the official maximum "moderate" amount of alcohol—0.99 ounces per day, equivalent to about two drinks—the industry would suffer "a whopping 40 percent decrease in the sale of beer, wine and distilled spirits, based on 1981 sales figures."[35]

The recent aggressive marketing war between Anheuser-Busch and Miller has prompted some candid statements about heavy drinkers. Early on in the battle to become the top beer, Philip Morris brought in new advertising specialists to pump up its 1971 acquisition, Miller Brewing Company. The first major change was dropping the long-time slogan for Miller High Life, "The Champagne of Beers." As *Advertising Age*, the nation's leading marketing trade journal, recently suggested, "The analogy cited the high brow tastes of the country club set who drank beer with relish, but while the tennis crowd tastefully downed a beer or two after a jaunt on the courts, they were not the *volume beer drinkers*."[25] (emphasis added).

The result of the strategy change is the "Miller Time" concept, which celebrates the toiling of the average working man. Miller suggests that its beer is the just reward after a hard day of cutting down trees or putting up skyscrapers. The

The beer industry's focus on the male drinker even dominates the low-calorie sales pitch. Miller "Lite" holds 60 percent of the light beer market.

predominant male focus of brewers is explained by Anheuser-Busch vice president for marketing Michael Roarty: "In beer marketing, the name of the game is reaching the male consumer. Seventy percent of all beer is consumed by 20 percent of the population, and it's male dominated."[19] Although 40 percent of women do in fact drink beer, they account for only a small portion of consumption.[25]

The beer industry's focus on the heavy drinking male even dominates the marketing of low-calorie light beers. The biggest selling light beer, Miller Lite, holds 60 percent of the light market and is aimed at men. John Collopy, an industry analyst with Robert W. Baird Company, said of Lite, "So they [Miller] decided to go after the high volume male drinker with it. They did all the he-man type commercials."[25] Collopy refers to the Lite Beer commercials featuring ex-athletes humorously debating the beer's "great taste" and "less filling" qualities.

Miller may also be targeting the male drinker with the intention of encouraging greater individual consumption. The Lite slogan, "Everything you always wanted in a beer, and less," means that Lite beer has the alcohol (it actually has a little less alcohol), but not the fattening carbohydrates of regular beer. Therefore, those who wish to can drink more. This may have a special appeal to the more vulnerable problem drinker, who is given a rationale for drinking ("it's only light beer"). Lite Beer seems to be digging up the ghost of the old

Schaefer Beer slogan: "The one beer to have when you're having more than one," which was clearly aimed at heavy beer drinkers.

Both the targeting of heavy drinkers and encouraging excessive consumption are advertising practices that violate the law. The Federal Trade Commission Act prohibits deceptive or unfair practices in or affecting commerce. In 1976, the assistant director of the Consumer Protection Division of the FTC, Richard B. Herzog, outlined for a Senate subcommittee the criteria for judging alcohol ads. According to Herzog, advertising which has the tendency or capacity to bring about any of the following effects can be prohibited under the law:

• encouraging drinking behavior to and beyond the point of abuse, including excessive and rapid consumption;

• encouraging those who are already alcohol abusers to switch brands by appealing to particular personality traits;

• reducing the incentives of those who are already alcohol abusers to take measures to control their consumption.[36]

Herzog also asserted that these criteria apply to advertising that either visually or in any other way presents or implies such messages.

One of the ads the FTC felt was targeting heavy drinkers promoted Budweiser beer. Anheuser-Busch encouraged viewers to "empty your schooner sooner" and to take "big swallows."

Scientific marketing studies done by various beer, wine and distilled spirits companies show that heavy drinker targeting is an intentional practice based on more than intuition.

A study done for Anheuser-Busch running from 1963 to 1974 was published in MIT's *Sloan Management Review*.[37] Professors Russell L. Ackoff and James R. Emshoff, both from the University of Pennsylvania, developed a theory of the relationship between drinking behavior and advertising messages. They refer to their work as "theory based marketing." Using esoteric behavioral and motivational testing, the professors sought first to classify drinkers into several personality types and then to describe how each type reacted to various advertisements. Their conclusions were intended for use in developing more effective Anheuser-Busch advertisements. Ackoff and Emshoff worked as consultants to the beer company and reported to the vice president for marketing.

Four categories of alcoholic beverage drinking were developed. A personality test was employed to allow the researchers to classify particular individuals in one of the four categories. Two of the four categories described personalities that try to escape social and personal problems by drinking alcohol. Eighteen percent of the respondents—and most alcoholics—were said to belong to one of these two personality types.

The researchers then hypothesized that the persons belonging to each drinking personality actually drink to become more like the personality type to which they belong. They refer to this phenomenon as "short run transformations in personality." To test the hypothesis, four advertisements were created to appeal with particular effectiveness to each of the four personalities. The researchers then showed the four commercials to a sample of 250 beer drinkers. After viewing the ads, the participants were asked to evaluate the taste of each brand. Despite the fact that the brands were in identical bottles and held the same brew, the researchers found, "The percentage that chose the brand corresponding to their personality type was much larger than one would expect by chance." Those advertisements that were designed to appeal especially to the problem drinker type did in fact succeed.

Ackoff and Emshoff also examined a sample of 2,500 beer drinkers from six cities and discovered that various brands of presently marketed beers have particular appeal to the different personality types. The researchers concluded that this information could be used to specify the target markets to be reached by existing or new brands, and that the information could be used to determine the kind of advertising messages that would be most effective.

Without further detail, the researchers said: "The understanding thus gained has enabled A-B to develop more effective advertising and other marketing tools at appropriate points before, during and after the introduction of new products into the market." Thus it is quite likely that ads based on the research did run. Recall that the FTC commenced an investigation of Anheuser-Busch, because of the FTC's concern that the company was pitching its ads at problem drinkers.

Dr. Marc Hertzman, the Director of Hospital Services and Associate Professor of Psychiatry and Behavioral Sciences at George Washington University, said of the Anheuser-Busch research, "In short, what they were able to demonstrate was that the common assumption in the alcoholic beverage industry, which is that some advertising leads to some more sales and consumption, can actually be made much more powerful by the application of scientific principles and the proper timing of when the advertising takes place."[38] Furthermore, the researchers applied their scientific capabilities to learning how to appeal to problem drinkers and alcoholics.

In 1975 the Federal Trade Commission objected to ads for Johnnie Walker Black Label Scotch that stated, "The road to success is paved with rocks. Let us smooth them for you." According to an FTC Staff memo (April 23, 1976):

> ...the ad appeared to us to suggest that Johnnie Walker was an appropriate mechanism for coping with personal problems. We conveyed our concern to company representatives at a meeting in November, 1975. Although the company disputed our interpretation of the ads, it discontinued the ads at the beginning of this year.

SPORTS PROMOTION IS ALCOHOL PROMOTION

Sports promotion is one of the industry's major marketing strategies, because audiences include high concentrations of heavy drinkers. The audiences also include millions of young men, another prime market. Sports promotion includes advertising heavily on sports broadcasts, sponsoring large and small events, promoting clinics, owning professional teams, using athletes in commercials, and sponsoring auto racing teams.

Anheuser-Busch (Budweiser) reigns supreme in the sports field, sponsoring 98 professional and 380 college sports events in a recent year – the same figures in 1976 were 12 and seven, respectively.[39] A-B claims to be the largest sports sponsor in the United States, dominating the broadcasts of every major sport. A-B also owns the St. Louis Cardinals baseball team, as viewers of the 1982 World Series were well aware. Miller has also recently gotten into sports promotions and is now spending $15 million to promote an Olympic Training Center in Boulder Springs, Colorado, and will also be the chief sponsor of the 1984 Winter Olympics. Not wanting to be forgotten during the Olympic year, A-B has reached a $10 million agreement with the Los Angeles Olympic Committee for the use of the Olympic seal in their beer packaging.[40] In addition, A-B's Michelob Light now sponsors tennis tournaments and clinics, and Budweiser owns the world's leading speed boat and a "land rocket" that is shown in company ads.

Anheuser-Busch is paying hundreds of thousands of dollars simply to get its symbol on a race car, hoping that investments like this will pay off in a big way. One A-B executive quoted by the *Los Angeles Times* says, "Hopefully, it will show up well. There's even a chance your guy will appear on the cover of *Sports Illustrated*. How much is that worth?"

Another marketing executive, also quoted in the *Los Angeles Times*, explained clearly why brewers sponsor sports events:

"People like to identify with sports heroes. If one is wearing your logo, they will buy your product because he does." Schlitz says that whenever a young racing driver appeared in his Schlitz-emblazoned outfit in his role as a guest television commentator, the brewery had a marked increase in sales.[41]

Hard liquor companies are also getting involved in sports promotion, such as Cuervo Tequila's $60,000 Redondo Beach Volleyball Tournament. *Advertising Age* observes that spirits' sports promotion is often targeted at the upper crust: Jim Beam's $250,000 thoroughbred horse race, Bacardi's polo matches, and J&B Scotch's $200,000 ladies golf tournament.[28]

Statements by beer industry executives and industry observers leave no doubt that sports promotion targets heavy drinkers. Anheuser-Busch group marketing manager Robert McDowell wrote an article entitled "How We Did It" for *Marketing Times*, explaining the beer company's strategy for staying on top. McDowell claims that sports promotion was essential for rebuilding the company and staying ahead of Miller. The heavy drinker is the key:

> We created a new media strategy to achieve a share of voice dominance within the industry and increased advertising expenditures four-fold with greater orientation towards sports programming to reach the heavy beer drinker. [42]

Anheuser-Busch marketing vice president Roarty told the *Berkeley Gazette*, "It was born of necessity—there was one thing we knew about the heavy beer drinker: he was a sports lover.... That was our target audience."[43] Roarty also said that sports promotion was basic to the brewery's growth in the past five years.

A recent comer to sports promotion is Coors. Slipping in sales, Coors raised its ad budget from $9 million in 1976 to $90 million in 1981, much of the increase going to a new 13-person sports promotion department. Coors is spending millions on local and regional sporting events like rodeos, racquetball tournaments, drag races, and bicycle contests. *Beverage World* reports that distributors are claiming that sports promotion has raised beer sales in various areas from 10 to 50 percent.[44] The Coors decision was based upon a "sports activity study" conducted by Westgate Research of Denver that identified sports events most watched by beer drinkers with "higher than average beer consumption rates."

Sports promotion has been developed by beer companies to rebuild or boost the firms' business. When breweries are looking for a solid marketing investment they go after the heavy drinker, as well as young men. The "heavy drinker" category includes millions of alcoholics. Thus, aiming promotional activities at heavy drinkers, whether intended to promote brand-switching or not, inevitably means that companies are encouraging alcoholics to drink even more.

The heavy drinker focus of alcohol marketers is clearly revealed in the advertisements placed by national and regional magazines and newspapers in alcohol and marketing trade journals. Numerous publications court alcohol producers to advertise in their pages. Because distilled spirits account for 85.4 percent of combined magazine and newspaper alcohol advertising, most of the inducement ads are aimed at hard liquor producers.[45]

The most common pitch in these trade press ads is that a particular magazine is read by an enormous number of drinkers and heavy drinkers. One such ad states: "*Playboy* men buy one of every three bottles of vodka, rum and cordial or liqueur sold to men." *Black Enterprise* says that their readers "have a higher usage index in almost every alcoholic beverage category." Another reads: "*Glamour* readers are 20 percent more likely to drink distilled liquors and 24 percent more likely to drink wine than the average woman." The award for bad taste goes to the Black Newspaper Network, which argues, "Black people drink too much. . . . Too much, that is, for you to ignore." All such ads boast of the publications' high consumption readerships. Some also induce ad buys for a specific region by claiming that the ads would lead to higher sales per advertising dollar in that area. As researchers in the *Journal of Drug Issues* concluded, "In this manner, an area already consuming a large of amount of liquor is reinforced and augmented in its habit."[33] Examples of these trade journal ads are shown in the following pages.

Moving from trade journals to consumer publications, some alcoholic beverage ads appear to be designed specifically with the problem drinker in mind. Some ads, placed in magazines with heavy-drinker readerships, encourage giving in to a drink or drinking excessively, as well as portraying alcohol as a relief from stress or problems. These are common emotional needs of problem drinkers and alcoholics. The alcoholic beverage is presented as the key to unwinding, forgetting your cares, and surviving. Drinking is the reward for the poor in spirit and the vulnerable, possibly heavy, drinker. The FTC's Richard Herzog said that "an ad would be particularly suspect if it suggested—frankly, or, perhaps, symbolically—that alcoholic beverages are the means of coping with social or emotional difficulties including loneliness, frustration or tension."[36]

Attention Alcoholic Beverage Marketing Executives:

American women make up 48% of your market.

You need to reach our 16 million to earn your market share.

Our readers are your best new market bet. Out of the total number of women in the United States who consume alcoholic beverages, they include:

- 1 out of 5 liquor drinkers!
- 1 out of 5 wine drinkers!
- 1 out of 5 beer drinkers!

We're FAMILY CIRCLE MAGAZINE, and we've got the numbers you're looking for to boost your sales figures:

- 16 million women read Family Circle every 3 weeks for our very real mix of active, attractive service editorial.
- Over 10 million of them are between the ages of 18-49.
- Nearly 9 million are employed, equaling ¼ of all working women in the U.S.
- The median income of the Family Circle reader is $20,000+, higher than those of all the other women's service magazines.
- 94% of Family Circle readers entertain at home, single or married, working or not. In small, medium and large groups,

many as often as once a week or more.*
- Buyers of Family Circle select all or some of the brands of alcoholic beverages in 4 out of 5 households.*

Family Circle readers are the consumers you really want to reach. But you'll miss them by confining your advertising to the traditional outlets. The self-styled "upscale lifestyle" magazines, the one-dimensional fashion/beauty magazines, or the elite special interest magazines with their limited readership. Not to mention the publication devoted to vicariously living the unrealistic, unaffordable lifestyle of that certain kind of urban "girl."

(And when you reach for Family Circle's 16 million women, you get a "bonus" draw of 2 million men — more than *Forbes! Fortune! Gentlemen's Quarterly! Golf! Nation's Business! Omni!*

Punch up your media mix with Family Circle. We give you the best shot at a great mass concentration of the valuable women's market. Remember: more consumers who read what we have to say want to buy what you have to sell.

Family Circle
A new issue every three weeks.

*Source: FC Research. All other 1980 SMRB

A New York Times Company

These ads, in fact, are part of the coping process. Breed and DeFoe have concluded, "Psychologically, the ads appear to feed into the alibi system and the denial mechanisms of alcoholics, leaving them vulnerable to damage."[46] Such ads justify the desire to drink as a relief from stress.

SAMPLE ADS

A recent ad for John Jameson Irish Whiskey is reminiscent of the Johnnie Walker ad that the FTC criticized. The Jameson ad states, "After the day's hassle and hustle, try a soothing change of pace." The ad does more than "suggest" that the whiskey is "an appropriate mechanism for coping with personal problems," to use the FTC's language.

The *Southern Comfort* liquor ad appeals to the need for relief, comfort and escape. The text directly states that the liquor is a means of "getting away from it all." The picture reinforces this message with an image of a distant and tropical beach. The man in need of relaxation is comforted by his drink and a woman at his side. He reclines in his chair and the woman, her well-exposed cleavage at the photo's center, seems to be offering herself to him. The ad also offers comfort in suggesting that "everyone needs a little comfort" – the alibi. Drinking is therefore ok when you are down, because everyone does so.

The *Crown Royal* appeal is simple and direct: the product will help the troubled "get it all together."

Steel Schnapps suggests that as a reward "after a hard day's work" one should have a drink. As a way of coping with the stress and strains of working, "pour yourself some Steel." That is, do *yourself* a favor, be good to yourself. This ad suggests pouring two drinks; another version suggests four drinks.

The *J & B Scotch* photograph appeals to the need for escape and seems to be aiming at the alcoholic personality. The exoticism of the ad offers distance from the observer's daily existence. There is a dream-like quality to the ad—"It Whispers"—which offers to carry one away from the current dreary state. The mist and the blending of the label with the lake add to the dreamy atmosphere. This kind of ad might be attractive to the heavy drinker personality-type which the Anheuser-Busch study isolated: drinking helps them into a state of little consciousness of themselves or their environment.[37]

Rather than appealing narrowly to the personality of the heavy drinker, some ads aim to increase consumption by encouraging greater frequency of consumption all around. These ads suggest to drinkers that many non-traditional occasions are appropriate for drinking. Alcoholic beverages should not be confined to dinner time, cocktail hour, or weekends, but can be consumed every day, after work, in the afternoon, or while working. Such ads clearly encourage daily drinking as a means of increasing consumption. The NIAAA considers daily drinkers to be problem drinkers and less than 10 percent of the adult population fits into this category. Ads that encourage drinking on a greater number of occasions are recommending and legitimizing potentially dangerous behavior. For this reason, the ads may serve as convenient, subconscious alibis for already heavy drinkers.

The *Johnnie Walker Red* ad is captivating and quite blatant in its purpose. The Johnnie Walker Calendar combined with the phrase, "Wouldn't It Be Wonderful If Every Birthday Ended With Red," clearly encourages daily drinking. It also implies that every day should be treated as a birthday and celebrated with liquor. For those who do indulge this often, it is "wonderful."

Similarly, *Michelob* recommends drinking all during the week, not just on the weekend. As a relief after work and the rush hour, the ads suggest that you should party with some beer, act as if it were the weekend. The slogan, "Put a little weekend in your week," means drink more often. This print ad is similar to Michelob ads on television.

Grand Marnier Liqueur's classy ad answers the question, "What time should one drink?" Rather than answering, "after a meal," which is the traditional time for a liqueur, this ad recommends the middle of the afternoon, "3:06 PM." The ad attempts to increase the occasions for consumption of a drink that has had a traditionally defined and limited role. This ad also promises adventure, elegance and style and makes no mention of the product's characteristics. Similar Grand Marnier ads recommend other times and places and, taken together, encourage drinking all day long.

Miller Lite Beer is presented in one ad as being useful while working and as a more-than-one-beer brew. This is especially significant since the ad appeared in a college newspaper. Research is fun, the ad says, when "you soak up as much subject matter as you can." The subject matter here is beer. Beer should not only be consumed while working, but one should drink as much as possible. When writing, the beer should be at hand, "a couple of mugs," in fact. "After all, writing is pretty thirsty work." This association between working and drinking is quite common in college advertising.

Whereas the previous ads recommended drinking on a greater number of occasions, other ads suggest consuming a greater quantity per occasion. It is likely that these also serve a legitimizing function or as a defense for heavy drinkers.

Sambuca Romana implies that one should have more than one drink—"The only thing better than one Sambuca Romana is another." This is reinforced by the visual image of five concentric glasses with only the last one full—presumably the first four have been downed. Unlike some ads with multiple glasses or bottles, this ad is not in a social or party setting. Rather the ad is aimed at a single reader.

Likewise, the *Steel Schnapps* ad directs its message at one person, suggesting that a good relief from work is a number of shots of the product. The text is written in the second person, recommending that you alone pour yourself the drink, not for your friends or for a party. And the ad suggests not just one shot, which is a substantial amount of 85 proof liqueur, but "some Steel." This message is reinforced by the illustration of four glasses full of schnapps ready to be consumed. The four glasses are for one person, "yourself." This Steel liqueur poster was found on a University of Maryland bulletin board.

Some ads not only omit any mention of moderation, but encourage excessive drinking by portraying in a positive light a disregard for control or judgment. Drunken behavior is depicted as a worthwhile goal of drinking. The ads certainly legitimize the habits of heavy drinkers and justify uncontrolled behavior. Such ads come under the FTC's restriction on ads which reduce incentives for controlling consumption. The Code of the U.S. Brewers Association holds that beer ads "should not portray comical drunks or revelry." The Wine Institute's code says that wine ads should not depict "any suggestion that excessive drinking or loss of control is amusing . . ." or "persons who appear to have lost control. . . ." The liquor industry's code is silent on this type of ad.

The two *Cuervo Tequila* ads are the most blatant. They not only recommend that people "Bust Loose" with their product, but they also portray drunken behavior as fun and satisfying. The male characters each have five women at their service, and everyone is having a blast as a result of the tequila. Drinking is associated with silly behavior and good times. This is all in contrast to the dreary 9-to-5 jobs these businessmen hold. Cuervo offers a relief and escape into a youthful, alluringly sex-filled, and wild lifestyle.

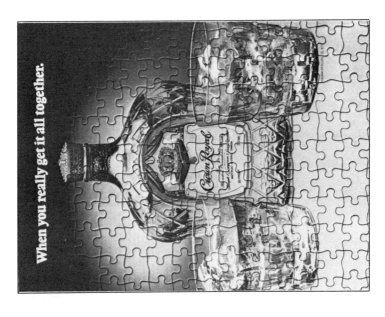

J&B. It whispers.

Steel has a clean, polished peppermint taste. Smoother and less tart than you'd expect from a shot of schnapps. So drive a hard day's or pour yourself some Steel. The 85 Proof Schnapps.

John Jameson
Imported Irish Whiskey

After the day's hassle and hustle, try a soothing change of pace.

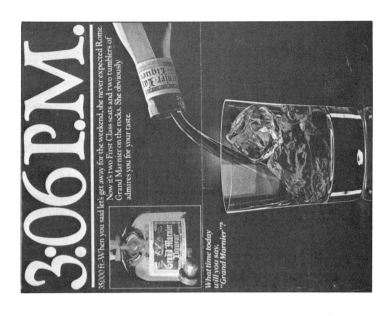

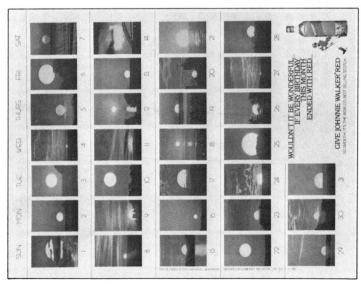

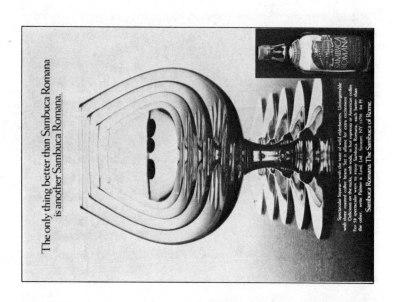

After a real fascinating lecture...

study the <u>real</u> taste of beer.

Pabst Blue Ribbon.

4.

*The goal "is to get the attention
of the entry-level consumer."*

Jess DiPasquale
PepsiCo Wine and Spirits International

Targeting the Young

Though every self-respecting alcohol company executive
would contend that his or her company would never, ever encourage a young person to drink, the companies shower vast
amounts of marketing dollars on young people – young adults
as well as those under the legal age.

Why companies cater to the young is no mystery: the biggest alcohol consumers are people between the minimum
drinking age and 34, with the greatest portion of beer drinkers
being between 18 and 24.[47] A large national survey conducted
for the National Institute on Drug Abuse found that 56 percent of high school students had started drinking when they
were in ninth grade or earlier.[48] The same study found that
41 percent of high school seniors had done some recent heavy
drinking, having consumed five or more drinks in a row within

Chart 4-A

STUDENTS GRADES 9–12 REPORTING USE OF ALCOHOLIC BEVERAGES *ON 10 OR MORE OCCASIONS* DURING THE PRECEDING YEAR

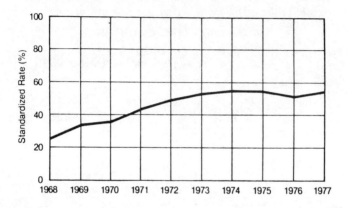

the past two weeks. As illustrated in Chart 4-A, the NIAAA reports that high school students who drink on 10 or more occasions during a year doubled from about 25 percent in 1968 to 55 percent in 1977.[49] The federally-sponsored Michigan State University study found that in one sampling of 115 ninth and tenth grade students, 24 percent consumed three or more beers a week and 18 percent had three or more mixed or straight liquor drinks a week.[50] Clearly, many young people drink and drink a great deal.

Youth drinking causes tremendous problems on college campuses, where drinking heavily is often seen as a badge of honor, especially in the fraternity set. College presidents are wringing their hands in dismay over student drinking problems, as described in a recent survey by *The Wall Street Journal*.[51] One poll found that as many as one out of six students consider themselves heavy drinkers. Two out of three undergraduates acknowledged that they drove a car while intoxicated. Drunk-

enness wa   campus crimes, including,
for instan   worth of equipment at a
chemistry   'lorida. Stating the obvious,
Dr. Jean l   ; University, told *The Wall*
Street Jou   lt problem. You have to go
across-current of an entire civilization."

Advertising to young people is more than just appealing to
existing drinkers. Rather, youth marketing is the business of
creating drinkers and brand allegiances. Contrary to the industry's rhetoric about advertising only to a market of confirmed drinkers, some marketing practices indicate a conscious effort to make alcohol a way of life for people nearing the legal
drinking age. Just as a 45-year-old person who abstains is not
considered part of the current drinker-market, 18- to 21-year-
old abstainers should also not be included. Nevertheless, the
alcohol industry either considers them drinkers by virtue of
their age or hopes to make them so. (Keep in mind that as of
January 1, 1983, only six states have a drinking age of 18;
another five allow beer drinking at 18.[52])

College campus advertising, ads in youth-oriented media,
and recreational packaging are all methods of attracting new,
young drinkers. To the companies, young people represent the
future and a potential for greater consumption. Researchers
of college advertising quote a marketing executive as saying,
"Let's not forget that getting a freshman [17 or 18 years old]
to choose a certain brand of beer may mean that he will maintain his brand loyalty for the next 20 to 35 years. If he turns
out to be a big drinker, the beer company has bought itself an
annuity."[53] As we describe below, all forms of marketing have
been unleashed on America's youth in order to make drinking a part of their life.

Advertising, in general, has a greater effect on young people,
including teens and children, than on adults. Young people
are open to a variety of images as they seek social acceptance

and clarification of their own identity. Adults are more set in their ways.

The great volume of alcohol ads in the media can have a gradual, but important, effect on young attitudes. Alcohol is presented as the social norm, as adult-like, sophisticated, and as a sign of success. Before even reaching the drinking age, young people are primed for a drinking lifestyle – we take drinking for granted, as Charles Sharp's remark, cited earlier, suggests. Former Federal Communications Commission commissioner Nicholas Johnson told a Senate subcommittee that "Young people drink alcohol because they think it is something that adults do. And there is no inhibition of advertising shown during hours when millions of young people are not only watching, but scurrying out to buy the products advertised as they are being instructed to do so by television."[54]

It is not necessarily the individual ads that can be so influential, although many are aimed right at youth, but the general atmosphere created by a steady flow of pro-alcohol messages. Charles Atkin and Martin Block, authors of the Michigan State study, contend that compared to adult respondents, adolescents:

- report higher exposure to ads;
- demonstrate more learning about alcohol;
- are more impressed with endorsements by celebrities;
- are more likely to perceive the ad models as being under 21;
- view these models more favorably;
- and are more likely to say they will get the product advertised, as compared to adults.

They concluded: "Thus, advertising seems to serve as a significant informal source of socialization about the subject of alcohol."[55] Like the media in general, booze ads inculcate susceptible young viewers with a pattern of social values – social success, wealth, athletic prowess, sex – which are all associated with consuming alcohol.

Analysts of alcohol advertising have pointed out that young people are particularly affected by the plethora of lifestyle advertisements that associate drinking with the "good life." Alcohol critic Robert Hammond, director of the Alcohol Research Information Service and editor of *The Bottom Line on Alcohol in Society*, observes,

> The youthful flavor of much of the advertising – particularly beer and wine – is aimed at youth. Liquor ads have the same kind of appeal to those just under the legal age, particularly when the stress is given to the things youths want the most in life – good times, social acceptance, and sex.[56]

The very existence of alcohol advertising has a marked impact on young people, as the industry undoubtedly knows. The alcohol industry is using a many-faceted marketing strategy to hook young consumers. As Jess DiPasquale of PepsiCo Wine and Spirits International said, the goal "is to get the attention of the entry-level consumer."[24]

Alcoholic beverage producers have developed college campus and young adult marketing programs to maximize the new-drinker market and to hit the entry-level consumer. This style of marketing hardly represents an appeal to an existing market. College sports promotion, special parties, rock music promotion, ads on late-night youth-oriented television shows ("Saturday Night Live" and others), T-shirts and other items bearing corporate symbols or ads, campus beer representatives, and heavy advertising in college newspapers and other youth-oriented publications are the major ways of appealing specifically to the young.

College campuses are concentrated and well defined markets. They are, therefore, choice settings for alcohol marketers. For one, the college is a drinking environment with over 80 percent of students imbibing some alcoholic beverage. Beer is the most popular alcoholic beverage, but CASS Student Advertising, Inc. found that 77 percent of college students also

drink some distilled spirits.[57] *Advertising Age* recently reported
the other attractive characteristics of the college market: it
is 12 million strong and expected to grow by 200,000 students
every year through the decade; it is affluent, with an average
annual disposable income of $2,200 per person; it is relatively
recession-proof since most college students are funded and pro-
tected by their parents; and it is a market estimated to be worth
about $30 billion.[47]

To reach this market, alcohol advertisers are penetrating
the lives of young people in innumerable ways. The major
breweries have been in the forefront of this movement, because,
as *Ad Age* suggests, "The most popular method of reaching
young adults—through entertainment—ties in so nicely with
a product like beer."[47]

Adolph Coors Company's marketing department explicitly
states that one of their beers, Herman Joseph's, is pitched
primarily to young drinkers. The company's "Marketing/Ad-
vertising Fact Sheet" (July, 1982) states: "The target audience
for Herman Joseph's is male 18 to 34 with emphasis on the
18- to 24-year-old." Interestingly, this youth-oriented beer has
10 percent more alcohol than regular Coors beer.

The person responsible for young adult marketing at Miller,
Kevin Wolf, confirmed, "We've found that athletic events, concerts and music-related events have a strong appeal with this
group and can serve as a way to reach a large number at one
time."[47] In addition, the highly concentrated social life of a college campus makes marketing easy. Mark Rose, the vice president for Marketing of CASS, said, "The campus lifestyle is one
that encourages camaraderie and interaction, and is a fertile
area for word-of-mouth to get going. It's a great place for
promotion."[47]

An integral part of the campus life is the college newspaper,
to which marketers give the highest "media effectiveness
rating" for reaching the college audience. Pabst Brewing Com-

pany's Bill Schmidt said simply, "The college newspaper is the key."[58] Alan Weston Communications, a college marketing service, reports that there is $15 million of national advertising in college newspapers every year.[59] Approximately two-thirds of this amount, about $10 million, is for alcohol advertisements, according to the *Wall Street Journal*.[53] This sum may not sound impressive compared to the over $1 billion spent annually on alcohol advertising overall, but ad space in college newspapers is much cheaper than in mainstream newspapers and magazines or on radio and TV. The dominance of alcohol advertising over other nationally advertised products gives alcohol a prominent presence on the campus.

Alcohol producers don't appear to be making any effort to restrict their advertising in college papers to states where the legal drinking age is 18. Some examples of liquor and beer companies putting ads in college publications in states whose legal drinking age is 21 include Miller beer (University of Oklahoma, *Daily*), Budweiser beer (University of Pennsylvania, *The Daily Pennsylvanian*), Jeremiah Weed bourbon (University of California, Los Angeles, *Daily Californian*), and Seagram's V.O. Canadian whiskey (the nationally distributed *Newsweek on Campus*).

In the case of distilled spirits ads, which do not appear as often as beer ads, college advertising violates the voluntary advertising code. DISCUS' *Code of Good Practice* states that no hard liquor ads shall appear, "in publications for schools, colleges or universities, or the student bodies thereof. . . provided that advertising in such publications shall be permissible in those states in which the legal minimum age is 18. . . ." If this were followed by all companies, liquor ads would appear in only half a dozen states. A small survey of college newspapers found 31 alcohol ads in 21 states where the drinking age is above 18; nine of the ads were for hard liquor. (Some of the advertisers may not belong to DISCUS or subscribe to the ad code.) It is most difficult to claim that such an audience belongs to an existing drinker market when many are under age and others just legal.

University of South Florida psychologists called the campus newspaper "a powerful socializing force on the university campus." Steven Walfish and his colleagues in Tampa examined alcohol ads and classified them as being neutral, promoting responsible drinking, or promoting irresponsible drinking. Looking at a week's worth of ads, they concluded that 135 ads (3,064 square inches) promoted responsible drinking, 124 ads (3,504 square inches) promoted irresponsible drinking, and 80 ads (4,449 square inches) were neutral.[60]

James DeFoe and Warren Breed at the Institute for Scientific Analysis, about the only other researchers who have studied advertising in college newspapers, concluded:

> We can only guess at the many and varied influences which affect student drinking patterns. But it is our feeling that Joe Cool-type alcohol advertising will not help students to drink more sensibly. We can all enjoy the fun of these ads but the underlying philosophy may be destructive for many students. Perhaps it would be best for everyone if Joe Cool stopped selling beer.[53]

Alcohol advertising generates much appreciated revenue for college newspapers, and many editors would undoubtedly defend alcohol advertising on the grounds that the income it provides makes the newspaper financially viable. But 22 percent of such newspapers do not accept any alcohol advertising at all, and an additional 11 percent reject some alcohol advertising, and still manage to survive.[61]

Slicker than college newspapers is *Newsweek On Campus*, an attractive, free, quarterly magazine "intended for college readers." *Newsweek* guarantees a circulation of 800,000 copies.[62] The September, 1982, premier issue carried ads on 18-2/3 of its 36 pages (52 percent). Four and two-thirds pages of this magazine were alcohol ads, including ads for Miller Lite

("Lite beer is like quarterbacks. We can't wait to knock 'em down."), Seagram's V.O. Canadian Whiskey ("You'll discover what might be the most refreshing drink you've ever tasted."), Yukon Jack liqueur ("The Black Sheep of Canadian Liquors. A one hundred proof potency that simmers just below the surface."), Old Grand Dad Whiskey ("So smooth, some people won't go anywhere without the barrel."), and Heineken beer ("Come to think of it, I'll have a Heineken."). Clearly, producers are not struggling excessively hard to avoid promoting alcohol among college students.

In their efforts to reach youthful drinkers, who are unconsciously developing all-important "brand loyalties," alcohol marketers know that young people read more than college newspapers. Consequently, youth-oriented magazines are often especially rich in alcohol ads, mostly for hard liquor. The September, 1982, issue of *National Lampoon* (circulation of 520,000) had 52 percent of its ad space devoted to alcoholic beverages. Nearly 50 percent of the magazine's readers are between the ages of 18 and 24.[63] Eleven out of fourteen ads were for hard liquor, a product that could not be consumed legally by many readers.

Similarly, *Rolling Stone*, with a circulation of 775,000, has an equally young readership: 52.5 percent of readers are 18 to 24, and 41.7 percent are college students. The August 17, 1982, issue contained seven alcohol ads, six for spirits. The September, 1982, issue of *Ms.* magazine (circulation 467,000) contained 15 ads for alcohol out of a total of 45 ads. The August, 1982, tenth-anniversary issue contained 31 ads for alcoholic beverages. Thirty-four percent of *Ms.* readers are 18 to 24.[64] (In contrast, three top women's magazines aimed at a middle-aged audience, *Better Homes and Gardens*, *Woman's Day*, and *Good Housekeeping*, with a total monthly circulation of 20 million, contained a total of one alcohol ad among them.) Despite, or perhaps because of, the heavy load of alcohol ads,

Ms., *National Lampoon*, and *Rolling Stone* did not contain a single public service ad to discourage drinking.

The liquor trade association, DISCUS, claims, "The industry is not trying to market a product which reaches the under age. Rather to reach a mature target audience...."[65] This public relations line clashes sharply with the reality of heavy targeting of young people by some liquor producers.

The voluntary code of the distilled spirits industry prohibits hard liquor ads in college publications, but is silent about ads placed in magazines with high youth readerships. The industry seems to think that it is unfair to advertise to people 18 to 22 only if they are in college. Whether in or out of school, this group hardly makes up a "mature target audience."

If anything, alcohol companies appear to be shifting their magazine ad dollar from general circulation to youth-oriented magazines. Atkin and Block counted the number of alcohol ads in leading magazines in 1977. To estimate how many ads the same magazines would carry in 1982, we counted the number in the September or late-August issue and multiplied by the number of issues per year. Our figure is only a rough estimate, though probably an underestimate, because magazines published in the third quarter of the year tend to have fewer ads than the average for the year.[66] In general, it appears that the number of alcohol ads in general circulation magazines has declined, whereas it has increased (sometimes greatly) in those read by younger (and heavier drinking) people. (See Table 4–1.)

For instance, in all of 1977, *National Lampoon* carried only 19 alcohol ads. The September, 1982 issue alone carried 14, for a projected annual total of 168. *Ms.* rose from 66 in 1977 to an estimated 180 in 1982, not counting the binge of 31 ads in the August anniversary issue. *Rolling Stone*'s alcohol ad volume will have quadrupled. Meanwhile, it appears that *Newsweek, People,* and *Time* may all have suffered significant losses of alcohol ads.

Table 4-1: **Changes in the Number of Alcohol Ads in
Selected National Magazines**

Name	1977*	Projected No. of Ads 1982**	Change
Newsweek	441	208	− 233
People	369	312	− 57
Time	365	260	− 105
Sports Illustrated	256	260	+ 4
Playboy	262	324	+ 62
Ms.	66	180	+ 114
Rolling Stone	44	182	+ 138
Sport	37	108	+ 71
National Lampoon	19	168	+ 149

* Atkin and Block[4]
** Extrapolation from one issue; see text

The beer industry has an almost exclusive monopoly on most non-advertising campus marketing techniques: sponsoring sports, rock concerts and parties, and employing on-campus student representatives to promote the usage of their brands. A short list of various events illustrates the big beer companies' heavy involvement on campus. Printed evidence of promotional activities is shown on the following pages. In the first part of 1982, Budweiser sponsored a Sorority Volleyball Tournament at the University of Tennessee, a tennis tournament at the University of Oregon, and a beach party in South Carolina for the college spring vacation. Anheuser-Busch also advertises on the sports broadcasts of 380 college teams. James Mosher, of the Alcohol Research Group in Berkeley, reported with dismay that Anheuser-Busch provides free beer to one and all in front of the student union before big football games. Also in the past year, Miller Beer promoted a Molly Hatchet rock concert at the University of Colorado and a Collegiate Team Olympics. Busch Beer (an A-B product) sponsored the

Charlie Daniels Band in concert at Southern Illinois University.

On November 19, 1980, Budweiser sponsored a beer-drinking contest at the Chi Psi Fraternity in Berkeley. A student wrote a paper about the event, calling it "gruesome and disgusting." ". . . [T]eam members gulped, and choked, red-faced trying to get the beer down. Three or four guys vomited in the bushes minutes after chugging the beer." In the women's division of the contest, the drinkers "practically inhaled the beer," but did so much more neatly and with less messy after-effects than their male counterparts.

An article in the *Houston Chronicle* explored the role of the campus representative. "To be a beer representative, all you have to do is when you hear an organization is going to have a party, you make contact and offer them free publicity, free trophies, free prizes, and financial assistance," said Coors' man on campus at the University of Houston.

One beer industry spokesman said that Miller Brewing Company really opened up college marketing with its "Pick 'em Up and Win" contests, which offered students prizes for turning in empty cans and kegs of Miller beer. A key thing about the contest was that the prizes were geared to group living situations, rather than individuals. The TV sets and pool tables encouraged whole fraternities to make Miller their beer.

Coors is generous with students, the rep says, because "students are a market. Budweiser is more generous than we are," he admitted.

At Texas Southern University, the student program coordinator told the *Chronicle*, "Beer companies come through for everything—for senior class picnics, for after-the-game dances, for pep rallies, and for tail-gating parties that precede the games. . . . Campus life wouldn't be as much fun without beer," the coordinator said.

Pabst and Schlitz picked up on the idea and have both been

BUSCH The official beer of The Charlie Daniels Band.

Busch Beer (Anheuser-Busch) sponsored the Charlie Daniels Band in concert on several college campus. This ad appeared in the *Johns Hopkins Newsletter*.

running sweepstakes. Pabst offered $13,000 in tuition fees and Schlitz promised pool tables, TV sets and other recreational equipment to college organizations like fraternities. To be eligible for Schlitz's sweepstakes, contestants had to send in emptied cases of the brewery's six brands—just a small incentive to drink heavily. *Advertising Age* reported that Pabst and Schlitz were "Fighting to make comebacks by winning the business of people just entering the beer market."[67] In late 1982, Schlitz sponsored a sweepstakes, which was publicized by The Who rock band. Winners of this promotion received trips to Toronto to hear The Who, cassette players, record albums, and Schlitz T-shirts.

The booze merchants have a dozen other ploys to promote brand recognition and college drinking.

In fall, 1982, Pabst distributed posters with a cartoon-like montage of campus life, showing students "Studyin' with the real taste of beer." Pabst spokesman, Bill Schmidt, explained that his company is investing its college promotion money in posters, because students hung them in their room for months at a time. Nothing like moving little billboards right into people's living quarters! Bud has sponsored a bumper sticker contest for "gutsy and bold" students. Monte Alban tequila offered a "wild west vacation" to the winner of its contest, and Seagram's 7 Crown whiskey sells T-shirts and memo boards.

Budweiser, Miller, Stroh, Pabst, and other companies have student representatives on college campuses to facilitate the flow of their brew. They are responsible for setting up parties, beer chugging contests, and campus taste tests and making sure that their brand is well represented and properly displayed. The reps also serve as liaisons between the companies and the campuses, acting as the on-site person for concerts and events. Tasks like on-campus postering and placing announcements in newspapers are handled by the representatives. That person also serves as a source of campus information for mar-

Both Budweiser and Miller sponsor ads in college newspapers touting local athletes or team successes. The individual named in the Miller ad, Tom Epes, is the brewer's campus representative at Georgetown University in Washington, D.C.

keters who design ads and promotional campaigns for specific schools. Budweiser, for instance, sponsors "Athlete of the Week" ads in many college newspapers–traditional Bud ads with a picture of an outstanding campus performer and a short description of his or her feat. Miller also runs sports-related ads adjusted for each school; one such ad congratulates a basketball team for making it to the championship tournament.

The campus beer representatives–who are either paid a salary of up to several hundred dollars a month or receive a commission–help make beer a familiar part of the normal campus lifestyle. As one ad in the University of Hawaii paper asks, "Having a Party? See Chuck Parker, Your Budweiser Campus Representative. Call Chuck at 732-6305 for your beer needs right on campus." The varied efforts of brewers to encourage

young people to drink their brand of beer fly in the face of the
U.S. Brewers Association ad code: "Brewers should not aim
their advertising at the young."

Playboy's "College Expo," a five-day spring vacation party
and commercial venture at Florida's Daytona Beach, illustrates the extent to which alcoholic beverage marketers in-
filtrate the lives of college students. The announcement for the
1983 event depicted College Expo as "the biggest college consumer show in the world . . . an outstanding opportunity for
you to boost brand-awareness, give a new brand a head start,
add new vigor to established brands, generate product trial
through sampling programs."

The March, 1982, "expo" activities were announced in a
special *Playboy* publication, *Spring Break*, designed for and
distributed to college students.[68] The 32-page, full-color, ad-
packed magazine called the event the "World's Biggest College Party," a bash "that really delivers on the goods." It turns
out that many of the "goods" that an estimated 300,000 students flocked to receive were brewed, fermented, and distilled.

Of the 26 events previewed in *Spring Break*, 17 were sponsored by alcohol companies, 11 of which were hard liquor firms.
Many of the activities were sports, but there were also tasting
parties put on by Yukon Jack whiskey and Frangelico liqueur.
Heineken hired some *Playboy* bunnies, while Seagram sponsored a dating game that "became more risque in its line of
questioning as the afternoon progressed," according to a follow-
up article in *Advertising Age*.[69] Many of the prizes were T-shirts
and bicycles, but there was also a campus party offered by Coco
Lopez drink mixes.

The dominant appeal was the drinking that would be done.
The preview said that one would be able to "check out new products, sample great new drinks" and "try your skill at downing
the Red Baron, a delightful new drink." The tasting is allegedly
monitored to prevent excessive drinking, and youths are ad-

vised to visit a booth on moderate drinking (no *Playboy* bunnies here, we bet!), but we imagine that the students can cope with these mild impediments to inebriation quite handily.

Spring Break included many pictures of students surrounded by drinks. Of the 14 advertisements in *Spring Break*, 12 were for alcoholic beverages: six for beer, five for spirits and one for wine. There was not one ad for another beverage or food. Alcohol was the main enticement and, it appears, the main event. In a state in which the legal drinking age is 19, the sponsors of College Expo are obviously promoting drinking among the many under-age participants in the activities. We have reproduced an excerpt of *Spring Break* on the following pages.

A study done at the 1981 Expo showed that the attending crowd included many young and heavy drinkers. The average age was 20, with half the students either freshman or sophomores.[70] An average of 88 percent of those who came said they drank, and 35 percent claimed they drank six or more cans of beer or six or more 1-1/2-ounce spirits drinks per drinking occasion.[70] The participants in Expo could hardly be considered a mature, moderate-drinker market. These targets of industry's marketing campaigns were young, many under-age in their home or school states, and big drinkers.

The College Expo event was sponsored by College Marketing and Research Corporation, a division of Playboy Enterprises. The same corporation has brought alcohol to college students in other ways, also. According to an account in *The New York Times* (Dec. 26, 1974),

> Now one of C.M.R.'s major activities is giving on-campus liquor tasting parties. It gave 400 of them last year, the biggest being for 4,000 at a homecoming at Florida State where the only drink served was a Mexican Sunrise with Jose Cuervo tequila...

A spokesperson for C.M.R. has said that recent concern about drunk driving has caused alcohol companies to tone down their

Another key market for the booze merchants is the military. Millions are spent promoting alcoholic beverages to this highly concentrated young audience.

marketing efforts somewhat. They are shifting away from liquor tasting parties (partly because colleges are forbidding them) and toward T-shirts and other premiums. C.M.R.'s Brian Murphy said that companies like using college students as 'walking billboards' to reinforce brand recognition. Murphy said companies are attracted to youth marketing, because young people who buy a particular product 'may stick to the brand for the rest of their life'.[71] Apparently the shift away from free booze has not affected Anheuser-Busch, because its 1983 *Spring Break* guide lures students with female skin and free Budweiser Light beer in three Florida cities.

The intent and effect of these promotional activities is to make alcohol an integral part of the college experience. All the major campus social activities, sports, music and parties, are surrounded by beer and spirits ads and promotions. While the college presidents wonder what to do about student alcohol abuse, the industry is busy preying on this market and its heaviest drinkers.

One reason that alcohol marketers have developed so many types of special promotion activities aimed at youths is that teen-agers watch less television than adults. Other media must be employed to reach teens. Stacey Lippman, who has been the ad director for Coke ads at McCann-Erickson says, ". . . the youth market continues to be the primary market segment [for soft drinks]. On the basis of that, we decided that Coca-Cola must be associated with rock and roll music."[23] Jay Coleman, a New York City ad agent explains, "Music is the most integral part of a young adult's lifestyle today."[47] Alcohol companies have been attracted to rock music for exactly the same reason. How ironic it is that straight-laced corporate executives are tying in with many of the same rock stars whose music and lifestyle they probably detest and from which they try to protect their children.

A number of major brewers sponsor regional and national

bands. Mateus wine has also sponsored concerts. Miller beer has recently joined in and is focusing primarily on advertising for regional rock bands. Ad agent Gary Reynolds explains Miller's decision: "Many of the regional acts have established themselves and have as much impact on young consumers as national acts who come through only once or twice a year."[72] Rock promotion includes celebrity endorsements, T-shirt and poster give-aways, and advertising for the concerts themselves.

Rock concert audiences can be quite young, younger than the "young adults" sponsors talk about. The public relations office of the Nassau Coliseum on Long Island says that at concerts held there, 55 percent of the crowd is under 18.[74] Don Kirshner Entertainment Corporation, a leading management and promotion firm, says that the *average* age at a concert is 18.[74] And Warner Brothers Record Company in California says that the age range at most concerts is from 15 to 21.[75] Although music is indeed a key part of young adult lives, concerts are more appealing to even younger people. As a Warner Brothers publicist said, "Younger people go to more rock concerts because they're just starting out and it's very exciting. They're less picky."[75] Of course, the age distribution at any particular concert depends to a great extent on the particular performers.

Schlitz Beer sponsored "The Who," a rock group, on a recent nationwide tour. Ironically, the Who's lead guitarist/songwriter is a recovered alcoholic and the former lead drummer died after overdosing on a drug he took to combat alcoholism.

Bull malt liquor (Schlitz) commercials feature both black and white rock groups. Pictured here are Tommy James and the Shondells and Kool and the Gang. Young people are a prime target for such ads.

Rock music-oriented alcohol promotion is also a major part of radio advertising. Beer companies advertise heavily on popular music stations with ads that meld into the programming. Miller Beer, for example, has several popular recording stars perform short songs as part of their radio ads. It is often difficult to distinguish the ads from the music, especially when the singer is Jimmy Buffett or Dave Mason. The songs are all tagged with the phrase, "If you've got the time, Miller's got the beer." Similar ads are designed for country and black music stations. As with rock concerts, popular music ads reinforce alcohol as a normal part of the young lifestyle.

Perhaps the most misguided marriage of alcohol and rock music is that between Schlitz beer and The Who, one of the most popular bands. As an article in the *Chicago Tribune* pointed out, the Who's lead guitarist/songwriter, Pete Townshend, is a recovered alcoholic. Keith Moon, The Who's lead drummer died after over-dosing on a drug he was taking to combat alcoholism. In 1979, 11 people died in a stampede

Blues singer Leon Redbone floats through an engaging 60-second spot for Budweiser beer. The commercial seems geared for the college crowd and airs on late-night weekend television.

that occurred at a Who concert in Cincinnati after a drunk fan threw a whiskey bottle through a glass door. What an example to our teen-agers, this ill-starred mix of music and alcohol. Recent Schlitz malt liquor commercials featured other popular music groups, including Tommy James and the Shondells, The Average White Band, The Four Tops, and Kool and the Gang. Running spots featuring these groups during college basketball games indicated clearly that Schlitz was clearly not trying to avoid advertising to college students.

MARKETING TO MINORS

The effect of alcohol advertising on children three to 18 years of age deserves special attention. While we do not suggest that producers are intentionally aiming their ads at grammar school children, it is obvious that ads can have both intended and unintended effects; they can reach primary targets, secondary targets, and unintended targets. Such is the case with television advertising.

Although there are some specific children's shows and specific adult shows, most TV shows are watched by young and old alike. Therefore, alcohol marketers cannot as easily target a certain viewing audience for their commercials as they can with magazines. As Robert Hammond of the Alcohol Research and Information Service told a Senate committee investigating alcohol advertising, "Print media may appeal to selected markets, but the radio and television airwaves can make no such selection of those who listen and view. Here is where youth, and others, who should not be the target of [alcohol] ads are virtually a captive audience."[56]

Given the susceptibility of youth to advertising, alcohol advertising on television significantly contributes to the general attitude that drinking is a healthy activity and the norm for our society. Mary Alice White, professor of psychology and director of the electronic learning laboratory at Columbia Teachers College, said, "Common sense would suggest that all the drinking and alcohol commercials on television would lead a child to believe that drinking is part of grown-up life.

Growing up on a steady diet of thousands of beer and wine ads is likely to encourage children to form a view of adult life in which alcohol is an integral part of virtually all happy occasions.

Alcohol is the most common social lubricant and the panacea for personal problems on many popular TV shows and in the movies. Drinking on shows complements the alcohol advertising and is viewed by young and old alike.

Unfortunately, it is virtually impossible to conduct a study to test this."[76]

Youth viewership of television during heavy advertising periods is massive. The examples that follow are only approximate, because the data are from 1977. Nonetheless, the findings are significant for our purposes. Sixty-eight percent of alcohol ads are shown during prime time (8 to 11 p.m. weeknights).[77] At that time, 31 million young people ages two to 17 watch TV, making up 22.7 percent of the total audience.[24] Nineteen million are two to 11 (children) and 12 million are 12 to 17 (teenagers). Another 29.7 percent of commercials for alcohol are aired during Saturday and Sunday daytime, mostly during sporting events. CBS Television reports that the average football game is viewed by 1.9 million children and 1.7 million teenagers, 14.6 percent of the total audience.[78] NBC Television reports that one million children and 900,000 teenagers watch the average sports event on its network, 15.5 percent of the audience.[79] The remaining 2.3 percent of commercials appear during the daytime on weekdays.

These numbers illustrate the widespread exposure of youths to alcohol advertising. Even if the youth audience is not the majority of the total audience, its size is awesome. The number of children and teenagers watching television far exceeds the adult readership of most magazines and newspapers. Of course, the alcoholic beverage producers are not responsible for the size of the television audience, but they surely are aware of the age make-up of their target audiences. No one can pretend that children below legal drinking age are free from the influence of slick, entertaining, persuasive alcohol commercials.

Now, merely seeing a beer commercial on television will not cause a child to rush out and steal a beer from the refrigerator or attempt to buy some wine at the supermarket. But the thousands and thousands of commercials that children see at an age when they are forming their conceptions of society will have an impact and will lead children to associate beer and wine with good times, relaxation, friends, and success.

In addition to the ads, there is the matter of the programs. A major report published in 1982 by the National Institute of Mental Health (NIMH) estimated that:

> conservatively, a child during an average day's viewing would see 10 episodes involving drinking, adding up to about 3,000 times a year. And this is not just casual drinking. In 40 percent of prime time programs, it is heavy drinking — five or more drinks — and an additional 18 percent of the programs depict chronic drinkers. . . . The drinkers are not the villains or the bit players; they are the good, steady, likable characters.[80]

The NIMH report concluded that "the widespread consumption of alcoholic beverages on television, together with the fact that such consumption is presented as a pleasant aspect of social life with no deleterious consequences, may also be fostering attitudes and subsequent behavior that reinforce the use of alcohol by viewers." Drinking is made the norm. And never is the child viewer reminded that approximately one out of 20 people who choose to drink will become addicted to alcohol, with all the disastrous consequences.

SAMPLE ADS

Much advertising, especially that on radio and television, has a general impact on the young, creating a positive social image of alcohol in their minds. Lifestyle ads which feature youthful-looking characters, celebrities, and sexual overtones may also have a special effect on young people. In addition, though, some advertisements are created specifically for a young audience and appear in youth-oriented publications. These ads target those nearing and just above the legal drinking age. Ads in college newspapers obviously are created with the student in mind. Such ads make up only a small percentage of all alcohol advertising. Nevertheless, they do illustrate the alcohol industry's interest in grabbing the young.

National Media. *Budweiser*'s humorous ad, judging from the setting, is geared to a college or high school age audience. The scene is a school locker room, not a private sports club where one would find an older crowd. The opened locker has a sports clipping taped inside, suggestive of a student's locker. The age of the characters could range from 16 to 21 (we suspect that models are often chosen on the basis of having an indeterminate age, appearing young to young people and older to older people). The Michigan State University study found that "younger respondents are more likely than older respondents to consider the characters to be young."[81] In addition, it found that: "Young people give higher ratings to the ads with young characters and feel more favorable toward the product as well; in particular, they are significantly more likely to say they will get the product."[82]

The characters in the *Lowenbrau* ad look even younger. The women (girls?) are exceptionally young looking. The banner and photos in the inset photo are suggestive of a college pub or dorm room. The characters are indeed young college students. The activity certainly suggests adolescent behavior. The beer is portrayed as the sign of friendship and camaraderie among school chums. The brewers' association's ad code stipulates that "beer advertising should neither portray nor encourage drinking by young people."

Cuervo Tequila's advertisement adds the sex appeal to the youth formula. Again the characters are young looking, a few could be perceived as under age. The drink is placed as the key to social and sexual success. As discussed, such images and messages have a powerful impact on the young.

The *Chivas Regal* ad is included here because of its use of a cartoon and because it contains an image appealing to children—a snowman. The intent of this ad is probably not to hook children into drinking scotch. Nevertheless, the cartoon and the snowman are likely to catch a child's eye. The absence of copy and the small print make this ad look like part of the magazine. A child is more likely to stop at this liquor ad than many others. The advertising code of DISCUS states that no ad "shall depict a child or immature person, portray objects (such as toys) suggestive of the presence of a child, nor in any manner be designed to be especially appealing to children or immature persons."

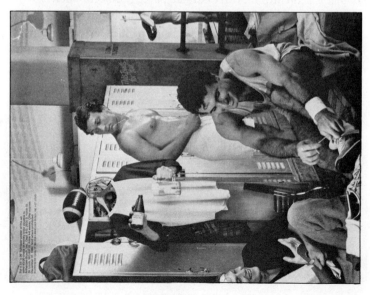

College Newspapers. As detailed earlier, alcohol ads dominate national advertising in college newspapers. In their study of college papers, Breed and DeFoe found 3,732 column inches dedicated to beer ads, and only 189 for soft drinks.[53] In addition to their quantity, many alcohol ads aimed at college students play on the emotions of students and project irresponsible attitudes.

Researchers reported in the *International Journal of the Addictions* in 1981 that of 339 alcohol ads studied, 37 percent encouraged excessive drinking.[60] The themes common to college ads deride education and promote alcohol as an escape from school work. Beer drinking is often depicted as "cool" and as the popular thing to do. Education, on the other hand, is a bother and a bore from which alcohol can deliver you. Breed and DeFoe write:

> Most of this advertising—especially for beer—is especially designed to appeal to the young and new consumer immersed in the strivings, frustrations, and decision-making that surround student life. It is important to note that these are lifestyle ads, created to make a wider statement about life and how to cope with it than ads which stress product quality only and urge the reader to drink one brand over another.[53]

As with general lifestyle ads, college ads make drinking the norm, and, in the college society, pressure to conform is great. In this manner, such ads play on the vulnerabilities of college students and reinforce behavior that undermines the educational experience.

Pabst Blue Ribbon mocks school as a bore and a joke and offers its brew as a serious break from the doldrums. The cartoon makes a complete mockery of the classroom and school work. Rather than worrying about the lecture, the ad recommends that students "study" the beer.

Carta Blanca, a Mexican beer, suggests drinking its beer as a way of escaping the tedium of school work. The ad also implies that drinking will get your creative or intellectual juices flowing when you draw a blank, a condition many students can identify with. Working and drinking beer are joined as a positive activity.

The same is true of the *Miller Lite* ad previously examined: "Great Writing starts with . . . a little beer." The beer industry's ad code states, "Beer advertisements should not make exaggerated representations."

The witty, double-entendre-filled ad for Hiram Walker's *Triple Sec* liqueur also places drinking before learning. The cartooned crowd of attractive college types praises the values of the drink. Not only will it "delight the student body," but one character claims, "No college education is complete without Triple Sec." The ad does admit that, "Secs won't lead to better grades. Just better times!" It is unclear, however, which the advertiser thinks is more important. Consider this ad in the context of DISCUS' admonition that "all advertisements for distilled spirits shall be modest, dignified, and in good taste."

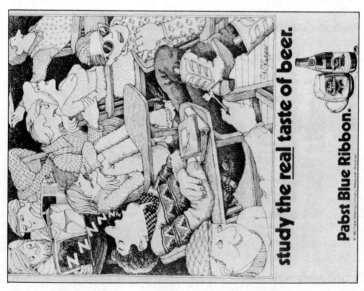

CREAMSICLE

For adults only!

43 Liqueur.
It's definitely not
for kids. Maybe
that's why the
Creamsicle* is the
hottest drink in
the coolest places
in town. You can
stir up the same
excitement at home:
1 part 43 Liqueur,
1 part milk,
2 parts pure
orange juice.
Then stir with ice and
serve in a tall glass.
The unforgettable liqueur
with the memorable name. 43

43 LIQUEUR.

5.

*"Today we consider any liquid
at all our competitor. We're positioning ourselves like a soft
drink."*

Frank Gentile
Senior vice president, Villa Banfi

Targeting the Light Drinker

In addition to targeting heavy drinkers and young people,
the booze merchants have introduced new products, new types
of packaging, and new strategies to further increase the size
of the drinker-market. Beyond the rhetoric of responsibility,
industry marketers and analysts view the light or non-alcohol
drinker as an important potential consumer – women and
young people chief among them. Analyzing the less than rosy
future of the hard liquor business in 1977, *Fortune* magazine
suggested:

> But they also have the perfectly benign opportunity for ex-
> panding total distilled spirits sales among the more than 84
> million adults whom sociologists define as light or moderate
> drinkers – people who consume as little as a few drinks a
> month. If half of them could be persuaded to take even one
> additional drink of whiskey a month, the industry would sell
> almost 2.5 million cases a year.[30]

This hardly illustrates a rejection of increasing consumption. The *1980 Liquor Handbook* recommended, "There may be thousands of consumers who drink infrequently not because they are opposed to drinking but because no product exists to satisfy their needs."[83] The clear intent here is to enlarge the drinker-market, rather than shift consumers from one brand to another.

The introduction of new products has played an important role reaching light drinkers. Light beers and light wines, developed in recent years, have been highly successful. The light beer market is presently 13 percent of the total beer market.[24] Lite beer by Miller, the original low-calorie beer, holds 60 percent of the light market and eight percent of the entire market.[17] Since Lite's success, most other major breweries have produced light beers, most notably Anheuser-Busch's Natural Light, Michelob Light, and Budweiser Light. According to *Business Week*, Budweiser Light is backed by $40 to $50 million in advertising, more than many brewers put behind an entire brand.[17] During the first half of the 1980s, the light market is expected to grow at an average annual rate of 10 percent.[19]

The purpose of light beer is increasing beer consumption, not keeping America trim. Although Miller Brewing publicly contends, "Lite Beer is not for a different drinker, it is just a variation," marketing activities and talk within the industry suggest otherwise.[7] A marketing executive for Anheuser-Busch, Robert E. McDowell, recently wrote:

> Miller used Lite to open up a market that other brewers had previously tried and failed. It took a diet-oriented product and gave it a masculine image, erasing taboos that existed toward low-cal products among image-conscious male beer drinkers.[42]

An industry analyst, Donald Rice, said, "Miller took a brand and created an industry."[25] This new "industry" caters to male drinkers previously constrained from heavy consumption by a fear of fat. Miller Lite has made it possible for more people to drink more.

Anheuser-Busch has taken this new industry and attempted to expand it even farther with appeals to women. The 40 percent of women who drink have consumed only 10 to 20 percent of the beer. Currently, however, about half the light beer consumed is imbibed by women.[25] Anheuser-Busch has taken the advice offered by the *Liquor Handbook* to create new drinkers with a new product.

The ad campaign for Natural Light and part of the Michelob Light effort are aimed at women. Anheuser-Busch group marketing manager Robert McDowell explains:

> In contrast to Miller Lite, Michelob Light launched a major print campaign to appeal directly to women. The bottle design, classy image and smooth taste appeal to female tastes. Print advertising depicts female lifestyle situations and appears exclusively in women's magazines such as *Cosmopolitan, Glamour* and *Redbook*.[42]

The senior product manager for Natural Light, Robert Merz, told *Beverage World*, "We decided to showcase a woman in a major speaking role in this new commercial.... Christine [Brinkley] exemplifies the successful, active woman of the '80s who is concerned about fitness and her appearance."[84] This kind of effort aimed at traditionally low consumption drinkers shows a clear intention to increase the market size.

A similar marketing movement is occurring with "light" wines – lower in calories and alcohol content. Light and "soft" wines have been introduced by many of the major wineries including Almaden, Beringer, Geyser Peak, Paul Masson, Taylor, and United Vintners Lejon. Coca-Cola's Taylor California leads the pack, selling between one and two million cases a year with an ad budget of $5 million. Its closest competitor is Almaden's Light Chablis with annual sales of 600,000 cases and an ad budget of $300,000.[25] Although these quantities are relatively small portions of total sales—Taylor sold 10.5 million cases of wine in 1971 and Almaden 12.7 million—many analysts predict that light wine will account for 15 percent of total wine sales by 1990.[21,24]

As with light beer, the industry hopes that light wines will expand the drinker-market. Peter Sealey, the vice-president for marketing of Coke's Wine Spectrum, said, "Light wine is going to do for the wine business what diet sodas did for the soft drink business and what light beers did for the beer business."[85] That is, increase sales and consumption by expanding the market. Sealey told *Business Week*, "Usually you expect a new product to cannibalize the existing products' sales by 70 percent. But because this [light wine] is a new category, it has brought in people who did not drink wine previously."[24] Margaret Stern, another Wine Spectrum vice-president, says frankly that low-alcohol wines "will fill a gap between soft drinks and wine and provide a bridge to bring soft drink and beer consumers to wine."[23]

Elliot Fine, president of Paul Masson, which has yearly light sales of 300,000 cases, said, "This product gives us an opportunity to attract those who are not regular wine customers."[86] Greg Sivaslian, Almaden's marketing director put it this way: "We are looking at the 33 percent of Americans that are potential wine drinkers. Getting new consumers through light wines—that could be an important prospect for expanding our base."[87] The intention could not be more clear: wineries are using their marketing expertise to boost the size of the wine drinker market.

Another means of reaching people, especially women and the young, who have not developed a liking for the taste of alcohol is developing product presentations that emphasize the non-alcoholic taste of a particular drink. Many distilled spirits are currently portrayed as tasting like fruit, soda or tea, and as being fun recreational drinks. *Advertising Age* recently reported:

> There is an increasing number of women drinking, and their tastes tend toward fruit juices, with which vodka and rum can be easily mixed. Although vodka has the same number of calories as brown liquors, it is perceived as a "lighter" liquor than bourbon or scotch, more or less complementing the general public trend toward low-calorie diet health food products.[28]

Many ads depict colorful and sweet mixed drinks or mixed drink recipes rather than the alcoholic beverage, itself. Other ads highlight the names and pictures of fruits that mix well with booze. One ad for a fruit liqueur says in bold face, "It tastes like real blackberry," and another reads, "Six fresh melons from Midori." These ads follow a 1977 *Fortune* recommendation that hard liquor producers should push "mixability" as a road to recovery. Like the low-calorie drinks, the intent here is to increase consumption. Alcohol critic Robert Hammond said:

> Advertising pitched to those who cared not for the taste of alcohol had much to do with the vodka success story. Vodka – through the screwdrivers, bloody marys, charley burches, wallbangers, et cetera – has been a major factor in getting women to drink and more women to drink more. This is one reason why women are becoming alcoholic at a rate that may soon make them even with the male population.[56]

The wine industry has recently adopted a marketing strategy to increase consumption by going beyond the limits of the wine market and competing directly with non-alcoholic beverages such as soda, tea, and juice. Wine analysts see competition with all other beverages as the key to growth. *The Wine Handbook* recommends, "Future wine marketing should minimize the intra-industry 'buy my wine instead of his wine' approach and maximize efforts to use wine more often instead of other beverages."[20] This statement not only illustrates a certain marketing idea, but also contradicts the industry's public position by proposing a retreat from brand preference marketing in favor of encouraging greater consumption.

The imported Lambrusco wines—semi-sweet and slightly effervescent—are in the vanguard of this marketing effort. Riunite, Giacobazzi and Yago Sant'Gria, among others, are part of what was called the "pop wine craze" of the 1960s and are now a major component of the U.S. wine market. Riunite, imported by Villa Banfi, is the third largest selling brand and Giacobazzi, imported by Renfield, is the eighth.[21,88]

As far back as 1976, *Fortune* contended, "Sweetish and generally fruit-flavored wines, sometimes slightly carbonated, special natural wines appeal to many new, young drinkers who have been accustomed to soft drinks."[89] The intent in marketing these wines is "to reassure a nation of chilled beverage lovers that nothing tastes better than a glass of cold, refreshing wine," according to *Business Week*.[24]

The marketing director for Villa Banfi, Sandy Johnson, said, "We no longer think of ourselves as competing exclusively in the wine market. The refrigerator, not the wine cellar, is the place to store Riunite, right next to the orange juice, beer and soft drinks."[90] Banfi's senior vice president for sales, Frank Gentile, confirmed: "Today we consider any liquid at all our competitor. We're positioning ourselves like a soft drink."[24] In a revealing remark, Pace University Professor John Gibbons, who is also a Banfi consultant, said, "The only difference between Riunite and Coca-Cola is that one has alcohol and the other doesn't."[90] Gibbons implies that Riunite and Coke can be sold to the same audience using similar marketing techniques.

His sentiment was also expressed by Margaret Stern, of Taylor California Cellars, in a newspaper interview, "There is no mystique about it. It is more a refreshment wine, easy-to-sip beverage." She said, according to the reporter, that light wines are not even intended to complement food.[91] In the same article Sebastiani's Billy Piersol said that light wines "increase the number of occasions at which wines can be drunk."

To back up wine's new recreational role, companies are now revising traditional distribution systems and packaging to reach the mass beverage market most effectively. Companies, including domestic firms, are beginning to sell wine in six-pack cans and short bottles. Yago Sant'Gria now markets a six-pack of short bottles, and Geyser Peak, a U.S. firm, is already marketing canned wine and is planning distribution of wine in cardboard boxes and plastic bottles.[92] Weibel Vineyards, the largest U.S. producer of champagne, has six-packs of champagne waiting to be released.[93] In this way, the wine industry hopes to open up the no-special-occasion market to its brands.

These new kinds of packaging help make wine more convenient and casual. New consumers, the beverage manufacturers hope, will turn to wine instead of beer or soda. The president of Geyser Peak, Wayne Downey, predicts, "It will introduce a lot of people who've never tried wine before to the wine business. And we hope they're not just going to buy the cans, but that they'll start upgrading to the vintage wines and the varietals."[94] *Advertising Age* said about Geyser Peak's canned wines, "The move is part of a company plan to carve out a new wine marketplace for itself among the estimated 80 million non-wine drinking Americans."[93] Confirming this observation, John Senkevich, Geyser Peak's vice-president and general manager, was quoted in the same advertising journal as saying, "We are trying to shoot for wine as a general beverage similar to beer and soft drinks, something people could just throw into the cooler."[95] In this context, it is worth noting that the Wine Institute's ad code admonishes against ads that "suggest that a wine product resembles or is similar to another type of beverage or product (milk, soda, candy). . . ."

Having already succeeded in getting wine in supermarkets

and convenience stores, various wine companies are now seeking to distribute their products at sporting events, restaurant salad bars, on airplanes, and in fast food restaurants.[24] Peter Sealey of Coke stated, "It is a long-term mission of ours to see wine in the fast food outlets by the end of the decade."[90] *Business Week* predicts that such a goal is not farfetched since most wine is consumed in the evening, exactly the time when fast food franchises have the most difficulty drawing traffic.[24] It appears that the wine boom may have just begun as increasingly aggressive, sophisticated, and well-heeled marketers invade the recreational beverage market.

SAMPLE ADS

Among their other efforts, alcohol marketers appear to be attempting to expand the drinker market by appealing to people who might want to drink, but do not like the taste of alcoholic beverages. Some advertisements portray the products as components of mixed drinks containing fruit, fruit juices, tea, or coffee, or associate their products with soda pop.

Such ads are common, especially in women's magazines like *Vogue*, *Glamour*, and *Essence*. On television and radio, commercials for imported Lambrusco wines such as Riunite and Giacobazzi portray their drinks as soda-like or "nice on ice," and the ads' general tone is similar to that pioneered by soft drinks.

The ads reproduced on the following pages downplay the presence or taste of alcohol and emphasize a fruit or non-alcoholic drink. Pre-mixed, canned drinks dubbed *The Club* are packaged somewhat like soda pop and advertised as the "adult" way to eat fruit (billboard ads for this product are similar). Likewise, *Arrow Iced Tea Liqueur* is the "iced tea for adults." Implicitly, regular iced tea is for children or sissies. A *43 Liqueur* ad offers a recipe under the headline "Creamsicle—For Adults Only."

Omelet? Shrimp Salad? Quiche?
At least the beer was an easy choice.

Michelob® Light
Compare the taste to any beer you like.

6.

*"We have kept looking for
places to find new drinkers...
Vodka has done all right with
women, but women are a big, untapped category for whiskey."*

— An executive for Brown-Forman

Targeting Women

Women drink substantially less alcohol than men. To a
health official, this is a heartening fact. To producers of alcoholic beverages, the situation poses a challenge. If only one
could find the key to unlocking this large market – as cigarette
producers have done so well, at the cost of tens of thousands
of premature female deaths – there are enormous profits to be
made.

John Powers, a senior vice-president at Heublein, Inc., sees
population trends signaling a rosier future for the alcohol industry. He has written:

> A number of demographic factors bode well for the wine and
> spirits industry. One is the emergence of women as a domi-
> nant force in the marketplace. More than 56 million adult
> women will be working by the early 1990's, a 25 percent in-
> crease over today. With their newly established indepen-

dence and higher disposable incomes, these women represent a huge potential market for beverages of all kinds.[23]

An executive of Brown-Forman, the giant American liquor
company (Jack Daniels, Canadian Mist, etc.), has said, "We
have kept looking for places to find new drinkers.... Vodka
has done all right with women, but women are a big, untapped
category for whiskey."[96]

In England, Seagram mounted a multi-million dollar promotional campaign for a new alcoholic beverage aimed at this
market. "Crocodillo is the first completely new drink to be
developed out of consumer research specifically for young
women during the last decade."[97]

For many years, depicting women in liquor advertising was
considered inappropriate. From 1936 to 1958, the advertising
code of the Distilled Spirits Council of the U.S., the liquor industry trade group, actually prohibited manufacturers from
using women in liquor ads.[98] Going along with the times, and
not wanting to overlook a large market, DISCUS changed its
code. The 1975 version stated that no liquor ad:

> shall contain an illustration of a woman unless such illustra-
> tion is dignified, modest and in good taste, and no such adver-
> tisement shall depict a woman in provocative dress or
> situation.

Getting women into ads went hand-in-hand with getting
women into liquor stores. As discussed above, light beer and
wine, as well as fruit-flavored mixed drinks, were especially
attractive to calorie-conscious women, many of whom do not
like the taste of hard liquor.

Some of the older women's magazines have a few alcohol ads.
However, many of the new magazines, like *Ms.*, which cater
to young, more educated women, are chock full of ads. More
and more of the ads are geared expressly for women, such as
the one for Michelob Light shown here. The ad, out of *Glamour*,
associates drinking light beer with low-calorie lunching. The

Budweiser's bloated $250 million ad budget enables it to target every segment of the population, including women.

women portrayed are young, attractive, and successful. Budweiser has been running television commercials that also feature women. The Ronrico Gold Rum ad shows a woman in a non-traditional role – playing hockey – and plants the idea that women should think of drinking something non-traditional, also. A product that is normally purchased or consumed by men could greatly expand its sale, if women were to use the product as well.

Gold Seal Catawba wine is promoted by an attractive male model who offers his telephone number (800-331-1234) for a "blind date." Viewers are urged to call the number and enter a contest. The winner receives a night on the town she is "not likely to forget."

CONCLUSION

Clearly, alcohol marketers are trying to get more people to drink and to get drinkers to drink more. Nevertheless, alcohol company executives and their academic consultants maintain in their solemn public testimonials and journal articles that companies are only trying to get people to switch from Brand A to Brand B. How terrible the executives must feel when they see *per capita* alcohol consumption rising steadily. One analyst of the alcohol industry, Larry Wallack of the Alcohol Research Group in Berkeley, observed wryly that only in the 'Alice-in-Wonderland' city of Washington do industry people have the chutzpah to contend that increasing consumption is not an intended effect of marketing. Even *Advertising Age* magazine noted: "A strange world it is, in which people spending millions on advertising must do their best to prove that advertising doesn't do very much!"[99]

PART 2: EXAMINING ADVERTISING CONTENT

We've been examining various marketing strategies used by alcoholic beverage companies to increase consumption. Let's now turn to more of the ads themselves and try to ferret out their intended targets and effects. Ideally, we would have teams of psychologists and marketers do in-depth analyses of these ads, but for the present we will have to make do with commonsense interpretations. Obviously, it would help a great deal if the producers of the ads would be candid and disclose the target audiences and intended effects of the ads.

For ease of presentation, most of the ads we shall discuss are from magazines. Therefore, the great majority of them are for distilled spirits, which are not advertised on radio or television. A number of the beer and wine ads presented here are print versions of broadcast ads. The disproportionate number of hard liquor ads should not be taken as evidence that spirits companies sponsor more inappropriate ads than the other branches of the industry, which make heavy use of radio and television.

SHARE YOUR GOLDEN MOMENT

E&J BRANDY

7.

Marketers want to appeal to people who "want to be like the people in the ads."

—*Charles Sharp*
Advertising executive

Themes Found in Alcohol Ads

Lifestyle. Frequently alcohol ads focus on lifestyle. These ads offer a set of desirable "outcome states" as the result of drinking. The ads are a promise of "making it" in society, if you only imbibe the advertised product. Drinking is associated with wealth, prestige and success, social approval, the leisurely life, hedonism, and sex. A certain whiskey is a sign of wealth, the correct wine represents class, and beer brings the fellowship of attractive young men or women. In all cases, alcohol is the key to success. The ads are emotional rather than factual, neither presenting product information nor suggesting control. The alcoholic beverage is the means to the "good life."

At a May, 1982, Senate Commerce Committee hearing on

health warning labels, advertising executive Charles Sharp
explained lifestyle themes in the context of cigarette ads:

> The ads are rich in thematic imagery and portray the
> desirability of smoking by associating it with the latest
> trends in lifestyle, fashion, and entertainment, as well as
> associating smoking with youthful vigor, social, sexual and
> professional success, intelligence, beauty, sophistication, in-
> dependence, masculinity and femininity. The ads are filled
> with exceptionally attractive, healthy-looking vigorous
> young people who are both worthy of emulation and free of
> any concerns relating to health and who are living energetic
> lives filled with sexual, social, and financial success and
> achievement.[100]

This analysis is equally applicable to almost all alcohol ads.
Those selected here to illustrate the lifestyle theme seem to
be more concerned with creating a general image than appealing to a specific target group.

The aim of a lifestyle ad is to get consumers to identify with
the image created. Marketers want to appeal to people who,
in Sharp's words, "want to be like the people in the ads."[100] The
impact of such ads is revealed in public attitudes about alcohol.
Block and Atkin found that 54 percent of respondents agreed
while only 27 percent disagreed with the notion that friends
have more fun together when they drink. Also, 45 percent
agreed that an evening out is more romantic when a couple
drinks.[101] Alcohol consumption is perceived as more than just
socially acceptable, it is actually necessary.

This perception may be quite profound for young people and
children, that segment of our population whose identities are
only partially formed. Young people are constantly seeking
role models and attractive lifestyles to emulate; often those
models are adult and in the adult world. Sharp told the Congressional committee that the lifestyle theme "is particularly
applicable to young people because advertisers are well aware
that young people seek to emulate the most modern trends and

project an image similar to those" in ads.[100] Block and Atkin also contend that alcohol advertising of this kind might prompt drinking by youth. They suggest:

> "Ads may reduce inhibitors that restrict the consumption of alcohol, by showing that the activity is socially acceptable and normative in society; ads may persuade non-drinkers or occasional drinkers to consume more alcohol, by portraying rewarding consequences such as romance/sociability, masculinity/femininity, and escape; famous or attractive characters in ads may influence impressionable young people to model their behavior."[102]

The 1980 wine trade handbook, *Impact: Consumer Trends*, suggested that white wine advertisers take heed: "In a society where young adults are now less interested in the counter-culture and more interested in jobs, social acceptability is important."

Alcohol ads, especially those using the lifestyle themes, contain few if any facts about a product's intrinsic properties and effects. In fact, little logical relationship exists between the advertised message and the product. In research reported in the *Journal of Drug Issues*, Warren Breed and James DeFoe found that only seven percent of alcohol ads featured a "logical relationship between stated intrinsic properties of the product and the goal-state suggested or implied in the ad."[103] In 88 percent of the ads, no such relationship was found, with five percent judged uncertain. In the same research, funded by the National Institute on Alcohol Abuse and Alcoholism, Breed and DeFoe found that only 10 out of 454 magazine ads contained an appeal for discipline or self restraint. Although a few examples of responsible ads appear here, they are the exceptions. Moderation is rarely the message. In the lifestyle ad, fact and caution are replaced by emotion.

The pictures and texts of the lifestyle ads reproduced here are quite straightforward, associating the various brands with wealth (*Johnnie Walker* and *Crown Royal*), personal class and success (*Martini and Rossi, Riunite,* and *Smirnoff*), the leisurely life (*Rums of Puerto Rico*), luxury and expense (*Myer's Rum*), and, romance and sexual success (*E & J Brandy, see page 102, Cruzan Rum* and *Tia Maria*), and athletic prowess and male camaraderie (*Michelob Light*). The *Michelob Light* ad is representative of many television beer commercials that feature athletics and male friendship.

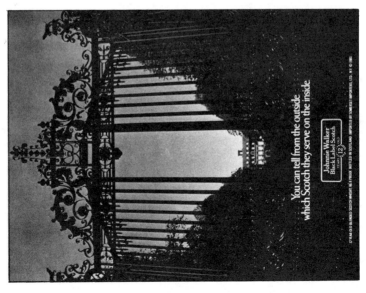

Riunite...like love it's pure and natural.

Cruzan Rum. The mellow spirit of the Virgin Islands.

Mellow. Smooth. Easy. It's the spirit of our islands. It's the spirit of our spirit. Cruzan White, or Cruzan Gold. The best-tasting rum under the sun. She tarries over Cruzan White in a Colada, Daiquiri or with cola. He lingers over Cruzan Gold on-the-rocks. Relax. All good things come in time.

Myers's. The first collection of luxury rums.

MYERS'S PLATINUM WHITE. Exquisitely smooth and born to mix. With a subtle richness that could only come from Myers's.

MYERS'S ORIGINAL DARK. The deep, dark ultimate in rum taste. The beginning of the rum taste. The Myers's Flavor Legend.

MYERS'S GOLDEN RICH. A uniquely rich taste inspired by Myers's Original Dark. Superbly smooth and beautifully mixable.

Myers's Rums. The taste is priceless.

Risky Activities. Dangerous activities are occasionally depicted in print and television alcohol ads, with some companies relying on this theme extensively. The ads show people shooting rapids, riding bucking broncos, hang-gliding, and working hazardous machinery. The activity often has a connotation of derring-do as well.

Risk-taking, or the desire to do so, has been cited as a prominent behavior of many alcoholics and heavy drinkers.[46] As part of living a dangerous life, problem drinkers act recklessly. The best example is driving while drunk. The risk-taking ads not only appeal to such personalities, they may in fact encourage such behavior. Advertising that associates alcohol with success in accomplishing risky activities may therefore be seen as exploiting vulnerable people. In Richard Herzog's interpretation of FTC authority, an alcohol ad may be suspect "if it portrayed behavior or personality characteristics that are distinctly present in alcohol abusers."[36] The FTC has also discouraged risk-taking ads because they may also encourage non-problem drinkers to engage in dangerous activities while drinking.

A distinction is sometimes made between ads in which characters are actually holding a drink while taking a risk and those in which drinking is just associated with dangerous activities. Either way, the association between alcohol and the activity is consummated. Block and Atkin, at Michigan State University, showed test participants various risk-taking ads and asked them for their interpretations. When shown an ad depicting a man skiing, superimposed over a giant liquor bottle, a plurality of 46 percent agreed that "The Lord Calvert Company feels it is OK for people to drink whiskey when they are skiing." On seeing an ad showing men fishing from a motorboat, 85 percent agreed that the ad was supposed to portray the fishermen as having consumed the product. And, 68 percent agreed that the Giacobazzi company feels it is OK for people to drink wine when they are in a rowboat.[104] These ads apparently triggered a link in people's minds between drinking and risk-taking.

The *Lord Calvert* ad is similar to the skiing ad discussed above. The text dares the reader to "Go for the Best," that is, be an expert kayaker, and drink Lord Calvert, the whiskey of winners.

Cutty Sark actually applauds those who take the challenges. Those who do, drink Cutty Sark whiskey. A glass of scotch is raised before images of death-defying human feats: diving, crashing, racing. The text acclaims the daring and risk-taking of one person. The "it" in the ad's ambiguous language, "Here's To Those It Inspires," could be referring to the liquor. Danger is the lifestyle of the Cutty Sark drinker. Never mind that drinking alcohol would further endanger one who participated in hazardous activities.

Although *Budweiser*'s hardy lumberjacks are not actually drinking, the association between drinking and using giant chain saws is apparent. Alcohol and a hazardous activity are linked. The superimposed hand seems to be offering the resting workers a drink. Although the characters are not done working, the ad still makes the offer, "This Bud's For You." The U.S. Brewers' Association advertising code discourages such advertisements: "Beer advertisements should not link beer drinking with activities and situations which require a high degree of alertness." The code prohibits not just actual drinking, but the association of beer with dangerous activity.

One *Riunite* ad presented is a story board from a television commercial. This commercial suggests that the wine is an any time, any place beverage, and encourages the drinking of alcohol in dangerous situations. In the first two frames pictured, p. 117, a couple perched on a rock in the middle of a stream is drinking wine. Accidental drownings are often linked to the careless use of alcohol. Another *Riunite* ad is from *Newsweek*.

In a humorous vein, this ad depicts a construction worker at the top of a tall building. He is being served a bottle of wine.

Riunite is a foreign product and is therefore not bound by the Wine Institute's advertising code. The code prohibits the "Association of wine use in conjunction with feats of daring or activities requiring unusual skill." In the world outside of advertisements, alcohol is related to a high percentage of drownings, boating mishaps, falls, and other "accidents."

An ad from the University of Iowa campus daily shows a motorcycle fueled by Heileman's Old Style beer "for a taste that will blow you away."

Sex. The sex appeal is probably the least subtle of all advertising styles. In contrast to the lifestyle ads that associate sexual success with drinking, these ads use sexuality as a direct appeal. Needless to say, these ads create powerful images.

The use of sexuality in alcohol advertising is particularly objectionable because of its impact on the young. Certainly the sight of a sensuous and provocative woman is attractive to the adult male, yet even he is less vulnerable than a maturing child or teenager. Block and Atkin found that respondents gave consistently higher recognition ratings to ads featuring suggestive poses. Products advertised by the sexy characters also attained higher ratings. In addition, "There is a sharp difference in response according to age level: those under 18 years old react more favorably to the sexual theme."[105] Whether consciously or not, liquor becomes associated with sexual pleasure and desire. The use of sexuality in liquor ads also appears to violate the federal regulation prohibiting in ads "irrelevant" matter that "tends to create a misleading impression."[106]

The sex appeal violates the alcohol trade associations' own advertising codes, although the codes are only voluntary and many of the violators—including many foreign companies— are not members of the trade groups. The Wine Institute prohibits ads that "exploit the human form," while the U.S. Brewers Association forbids ads that are "even slightly lewd or obscene." The DISCUS code encourages depictions of women that are "dignified, modest and in good taste." Both the visuals and the text of the ads depicted here violate the word and spirit of these codes.

As was true of the previous ad types, the sex appeal ads make little or no mention of the products' contents or taste and fail to suggest moderation. Restraint is the last thing these ads suggest.

The sex appeal approach is oftentimes blatant. The *Black Velvet* and *Two Fingers* ads rely mainly on visual impact reinforced by very suggestive slogans. The Velvet woman has a classy appeal – gold bracelet, opal ring, pearl necklace – and is supplicating the viewer on her knees. Her shirt is unbuttoned to her navel, her hair is falling loose, and she asks for some "Velvet Touchin'." The Two Fingers woman has a younger appeal – T-shirt and denim shorts. This particular ad was placed in the youth-oriented *National Lampoon*, among other places. The slogan, "Two Fingers is all it takes," is suggestive of sexual activity. It appears that the creators of these ads never read the DISCUS code, which asks that "no such ad shall depict a woman in a provocative dress or situation."

The *Campari, St. Pauli* and *Yukon Gold* ads rely more on the text for punch. They all associate drinking with sexual activity: "Tony Roberts talks about his first time"; "You never forget your first Girl"; and "The Bottle That Shows Beaver" (beaver being slang for vagina). The Yukon Gold ad appears to be a direct violation of the Bureau of Alcohol, Tobacco and Firearms' prohibition against "obscene" and "indecent" statements in advertisements.

Another ad making the rounds in 1983 promoted *Rumple Minze* 100 proof peppermint schnaaps. One boyish looking silhouette asks another, "Why am I not scoring with lady-type persons?" His friend responds, "Do you have Rumple Minze in your freezer." (We found this ad in Michigan State University's newspaper, *The State News* and Georgetown University's newspaper *The Hoya*, more examples of ads aimed at young people in states with a drinking age for liquor of 21.)

Many heavy drinkers and alcoholics have a strong psychological relationship with alcohol, replacing their mate with their bottle. Those addicted to alcohol certainly have an emotional attachment to drinking. Breed and De Foe observed the depiction of men and women in print ads:

> In one, the man is fascinated by the drink while the woman is equally fascinated by the man. The other pattern finds

the man and the woman relating to each other through the alcohol; both are staring thoughtfully at the drink. This rather problematic triadic relationship is not uncommon among heavy drinkers in real life.[103]

For people who are not problem drinkers, sex-oriented ads link drinking with one of life's most basic pleasures. Even for these people, the ads are deceptive. Recall the words from Macbeth:

"It [drink] provokes the desire, but it takes away the performance."

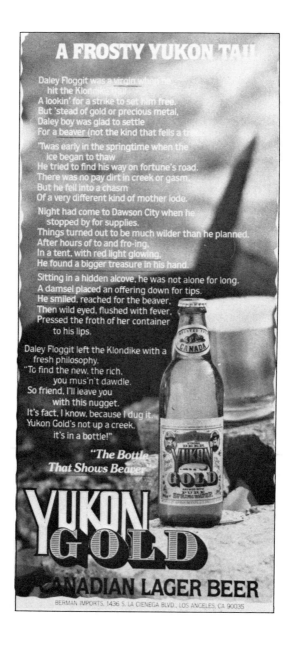

Taste. A number of alcohol firms promote their products as tasting good. These ads stand in contrast to the previous ads, which exclude any message about the properties of the product. The center of attention in the taste appeal is the drink, not money, tradition, or sex.

"Taste" ads are certainly less objectionable than those associating alcohol with sexual or social success. Nevertheless, they constitute part of the mass of alcohol advertising and contribute to the wholly positive attitude toward drinking that is pervasive in society. Never do they acknowledge the problems related to alcohol.

The *Natural Light* and *Paul Masson* ads are as responsible as one could expect. They associate drinking with eating. These products taste good and complement a meal, say the ads. They are not offered as any time, any place recreational drinks, or as a panacea for loneliness and failure. Finally, the VO pitch is straightforward—many Americans drink this whiskey because they like its taste.

Ahh, the beer with the taste for food!

"Unidentified Printed Objects." Some alcohol ads contain many swirls, squiggles, and unusual shapes, typically showing up in the simulated ice cubes and fluids. These elements have been dubbed by Warren Breed, of the Institute for Scientific Analysis in Berkeley, "Unidentified Printed Objects," or UPOs. The forms are more often distorted and grotesque than visually pleasing. With little or no imagination, one can see some of these elements as faces, animals, breasts, penises, death masks, and other forms rich in symbolism.

Some analysts suggest that these shapes were designed and used to appeal to the subconscious of observers.[107] Such speculations prompted the Federal Bureau of Alcohol, Tobacco and Firearms to propose a rule in 1980 prohibiting so-called subliminal advertising.[108]

The purpose of UPOs has never been explained adequately, though they appear to be prevalent and intentional creations. Breed and DeFoe found such shapes in 45.5 percent of the alcohol print ads they studied and found that they are far less frequent in ads for other products.[103] The frequency of UPOs and the apparent conscious effort of advertisers to create them indicate the need for further investigation. Representatives of the advertising industry contend that UPOs are mere accidents and not intended to have any conscious or subconscious effect on consumers.

The Puerto Rico rum ad depicted here includes UPOs in the ice cubes and liquid. Bruce Maresca, the account director for Puerto Rican rums at Kenyon & Eckhardt advertising agency, readily admitted that there were drawings of strange creatures in the ice cubes. He told the authors that he would look into the matter further (the ad was prepared before he joined the company), but subsequently refused to answer phone calls.[109]

Photo retouchers make a living doctoring photographs to suit the whims of advertising art directors. Quite often they draw strange creatures into otherwise realistic photographs.

The Exception: Moderation. Credit should be given to the few alcohol companies that publish ads that allude to the value of moderation and judgment in drinking. The most consistent example is provided by Seagram Distillers Co., which uses the phrase "enjoy our quality in moderation" in most of its whiskey ads. Breed and DeFoe found that two percent of the print ads they studied carried the moderation message.[103] In addition, especially around July 4th, Labor Day, Christmas, and New Year's Day, a company or trade association buys full-page magazine or newspaper ads to discourage drunk driving. The ultimate effect of such industry-sponsored ads, however, is meager, because of the ads' rarity, and, in some cases, subtlety. In isolation, when several ads are displayed at a congressional hearing, they appear impressive. In the context of a person's real life, they are simply drowned out by the thousands of standard commercials, ads, billboards, and other forms of promotional activity.

This public service campaign sponsored by DISCUS for Students Against Drunk Driving encourages young people to call home if they have become too drunk to drive. But the campaign is mum on the fact that drinking by teens is illegal in no fewer than 25 states.

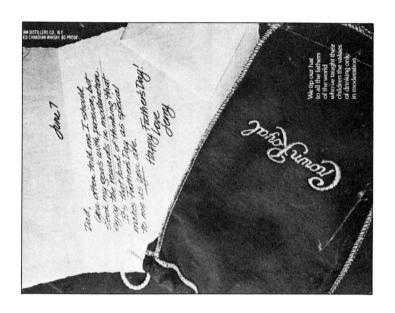

Michelob's almost wordless commercials seek to instill an impression of high quality in the viewer's mind. Most beers are almost interchangeable; companies rely on images created by advertising to "segment" the market and attract particular types of people. This ad promotes drinking, but hardly in an objectionable way.

Hanging out shouldn't give you a hangover.

Don't drink too much of a good thing.
The Distilled Spirits Council of the United States.

8.

The dangers of alcohol and the power of marketing have convinced numerous nations to impose significant restrictions on alcohol marketing, up to and including total prohibitions on advertising.

The Decision is Ours

The alcoholic beverage industry appears to have overcome its hangover from the grim days of Prohibition. Any reluctance to aggressively promote alcoholic beverages and encourage drinking has long since disappeared.

As we have seen, the industry is working to boost alcohol consumption through a broad range of sophisticated and innovative marketing activities. Companies inundate televised sports events with commercials. They sponsor rock and country music concerts from coast to coast. They distribute premiums that make half the college students in the country "walking billboards." Wine in cans, pre-mixed cocktails, plastic wine and liquor bottles, sales in supermarkets and gas stations, and low-calorie products all make alcohol more convenient, accessible, and attractive to an increasing number of consumers.

Some marketing activities are particularly objectionable, because they appeal specifically to youths or heavy drinkers or because they associate alcohol with performing risky activities. A disproportionate number of offensive ads, many emphasizing sex, appear to be sponsored by foreign companies. However, the objectionable details of specific ads represent only a small part of the problem. It is more important to consider the long-term subtle effects of *any* kinds of advertising and marketing for products as potentially dangerous and addictive as beer, wine and liquor.

We have cited numerous ads and marketing techniques that are clearly inappropriate, but many, if not most, advertisements are much less objectionable. Some beer ads, for instance, consist primarily of music associated with a particular brand of beer; many liquor ads show just the bottle and have but a few brief words of description. These ads would seem to be quite innocuous. Does that mean that societal action should be triggered only by particularly offensive ads, but not others? Hardly. Alcohol marketing must be considered in the context of the problems associated with alcohol: the emotional and economic devastation of careers, families, health, and the fabric of our society. The total damage done each year by alcohol amounts to over 100,000 deaths and $120 billion in economic costs. All ads, all marketing practices, are designed to sell products and encourage drinking. Therefore, every aspect of alcohol marketing must be scrutinized and confronted, for none can be considered helpful in reducing drinking problems.

Charles Sharp, an advertising executive cited in the beginning of this report, has said, "Drinking is something we take for granted, unlike smoking which is more an active decision. As a person grows up he changes from soda pop to alcohol."[16] Sharp's observation suggests that alcohol has insinuated itself into our lifestyle to such a great extent that we fail to recognize the consequences. In movies, television, and advertisements, drinking is portrayed as the social norm. Drinking is depicted as the appropriate behavior of the youthful, attractive, successful person. Alcoholic beverages are available in supermarkets, on airplanes, and at baseball games. If corporate leaders have their way, alcohol will be showing up in thousands of fast food restaurants.

Alcohol producers are legitimate and revered *Fortune* 500 companies. They sponsor concerts, college parties, and football games. It takes a special effort to recall that alcohol beverages, at least in theory, are substances controlled very strictly by local and federal governments. Alcohol producers have taken advantage of their legitimate position in society to boost profits through greater consumption. They have styled their ads, reshaped their packages, and done a hundred other things to persuade more people to drink and persuade drinkers to drink more, without any serious concern for the devastating effects of their products.

The dangers of alcohol and the power of marketing have convinced numerous nations to impose significant restrictions on alcohol marketing, up to and including total prohibitions on advertising. In Ecuador, for instance, alcohol beverages may not be advertised before 9 p.m. Switzerland forbids any alcohol advertising on television; India has banned both radio and television ads for alcohol. The province of Quebec does not allow endorsements by famous personalities, and Venezuela does not permit sports activities or athletes to appear in advertising. The province of Ontario has strict rules on the size and amount of alcohol print advertising in magazines, on buses, and on billboards. Finland totally forbids alcohol advertising, even to the extent of prohibiting news pictures that show bottle labels. Norway also forbids alcohol advertising, except in restaurant trade publications. New Zealand does not allow the use of brand names in advertising, but only such details as the names of retail and wholesale outlets, hours of sale, and address.[110,111]

Despite increasing concern about alcohol abuse, the U.S. alcohol industry is virtually unfettered in promoting greater alcohol consumption. The last serious congressional inquiry into alcohol advertising was a hearing chaired by Senator William Hathaway (D-Me.) in 1976. The most recent action in the regulatory arena was the Federal Trade Commission's 1982 decision to drop its inquiry into marketing efforts aimed at vulnerable drinkers by Anheuser-Busch and Somerset Importers. At the same time, the FTC decided against mounting a broader inquiry into what its staff said were widespread efforts by many companies to target heavy drinkers.

The voluntary advertising codes of the three segments of the alcohol industry may be well-intentioned and provide some standards, but they are woefully inadequate and widely violated. They serve as partial guidance for member companies, but are not binding, do not cover non-member companies, do not cover marketing activities outside of advertising, and are at times so vague as to be meaningless. In general, the codes are shaped by current advertising practices, rather than the other way around. Comparing marketing campaigns to ad codes, one can fairly conclude that such codes are mere window dressing and that industry self-regulation is a farce.

What can we expect from the alcoholic beverage industry in the future? Judging from the past few years, we can anticipate a wider range of ever more brazen and effective marketing efforts. "Effectiveness" means more drinking, along with higher profits, resulting, of course, in more alcohol problems. Consider the following:

• Advertising budgets are likely to continue their rapid rise, considering that major marketers of consumer products, including Coca-Cola and the tobacco companies, are moving so strongly into the alcoholic beverage field.

• In 1982, two liquor companies (makers of M*A*S*H and Cossack vodkas) together with several radio and television stations broke the longstanding voluntary ban on broadcast liquor advertising.

• The beer industry's Code prohibits actual drinking in television commercials, but the Code does not apply to cable television. In the first newsworthy deviation from the code, Budweiser beer:

> made history with a lively new commercial that shows young people actually quaffing the product. The spot was created expressly for MTV (Music Television), the rock network that began last November and immediately became one of the hot cable services.... There are reports that liquor companies... barred from broadcast television by the code, have made overtures to cable but so far have been rebuffed.[112]

The programming–and the Budweiser commercials–here would undoubtedly be attractive to minors.

• Seagram is finally getting its name on television by sponsoring ads for mixers. Though the mixers are non-alcoholic, the ads will certainly benefit the company's alcoholic products, as well.

• CBS announced in late 1982 that it was dropping the prohibition against drinking alcoholic beverages in commercials, though the network, as of March, 1983, has not run such commercials. This erosion of commercial standards will probably begin with genteel sipping, but eventually lead to quaffing and late-night chug-a-lugging.

• In late 1982, an entrepreneur tried selling "Nude Beer," an innovative product that was to feature bare bosoms on the label, changing each month like *Playboy*'s Playmate of the Month. This was going too far, even for some of the lackadaisical state regulatory agencies. The producer has gone to court to try to reverse the regulatory agencies' rebuffs.

• Despite increased public concern about drunk driving,

An Open Letter to the American Taxpayer:

Reducing the Federal budget deficit by stopping the abuses of the tax code and cutting Federal spending, is an important national priority.

The Congress, however, is unfairly singling out only one industry for a major new tax increase. A massive 36 percent increase only on liquor is being proposed.

Before Congress turns to major new taxes to reduce the budget deficit, there first should be an equal amount of real spending reductions. Then, all industries must contribute their fair share of any tax increase.

We believe that the liquor industry and its consumers are providing a fair share. Consider the facts.

■ Liquor is already the most heavily taxed consumer product in the U.S. 43 percent of the retail price is taxes.

■ The liquor industry already is suffering from major new taxes. The states have increased liquor taxes for the past four years at a rate equal to one tax increase a month. Tax increases in 1983 alone are expected to raise another $100 million.

■ Excise taxes, such as on liquor, are the most regressive form of taxation. They hurt middle- and low-income people more than higher-income families. There are no excise taxes on furs, private planes, yachts, and many other similar high-income luxuries.

■ The liquor industry already suffers unemployment and declining sales—liquor consumption was flat in 1981, down in 1982 and 1983, and continues weak in 1984.

■ The proposed 36 percent tax increase will cost an additional 18,000 jobs in the alcohol beverage industry—60 to 70 percent of the businesses in our industry are small businesses employing 1 to 4 people.

We believe that the proposed 36 percent excise tax increase on liquor is unfair and ill-advised. We urge the Congress to return to its stated objective of reducing Federal budget deficits through sensible spending cuts and tax abuse reform. Under any circumstances, all industries should be treated fairly. The liquor industry and its consumers should not be singled out to bear the brunt of a major new tax increase.

Distilled Spirits Council of the United States, Inc.

The Distilled Spirits Council of the United States ran this ad in *The New York Times* and *The Washington Post* in March 1984 to generate opposition against raising federal alcohol excise taxes, last hiked in 1951. DISCUS complained that its side of the story had not been portrayed fairly by the media.

some gas stations have begun selling beer.

• Trade journals predict the advent of electronically-controlled, laser-powered, three-dimensional billboards likely to be rented by alcohol companies. Giant plastic replicas of beer cans are already used as attention-getting gimmicks.

• The prospect of selling alcoholic beverages in supermarkets sets the hearts of booze merchants aflutter. According to one report, ". . . when wine sales in Idaho were liberalized in 1971, sales jumped by 283 percent the first year. Similarly, sales shot up by 718 percent in Maine and 165 percent in Montana when regulation was liberalized."[113]

It is critically important, but very difficult, to systematically monitor and analyze alcoholic beverage marketing. One of the problems is corporate secrecy. Only government agencies, using *subpoena* power, have the ability to penetrate the files of advertising agencies and producers. A major defect of traditional studies of alcohol advertising is that they focussed almost exclusively on print ads and ignored radio and television ads, the very vehicles that have the greatest impact on children and the general population. Video-cassette recorders in the hands of researchers would help solve this problem, especially if advertisers decline to provide the researchers with copies of their recent ads. The subtlety of the effects, the absence of good control groups, and the plethora of influences in a modern society are methodological problems that may be insurmountable. Notwithstanding these difficulties, we recommend that independent academic experts, perhaps with funding from the National Institute on Alcohol Abuse and Alcoholism and other agencies, pursue studies such as:

• an in-depth psychological study of how heavy drinkers and alcoholics perceive alcohol advertising and how they are affected by it;

• a psychological and sociological analysis of the long-term effects of alcohol advertising and how the portrayal of alcohol on television and in movies affects the way children view alcohol in our society;

• a systematic analysis by psychologists and marketing specialists of the content, motives, and likely effects of ads and other marketing efforts;

• a comprehensive review of the extent and effects of promotional efforts other than print and broadcast advertising;

• a study of the way drinking is portrayed on television and in movies, and the effect such portrayal has on public attitudes toward alcohol;

• a study of how alcohol ads affect non-drinkers;

• a study of the influence educational "counter-ads" and follow-up activities would have on youth perceptions of alcohol use.

Because academic studies can go only so far, we urge additional activities that might be conducted by governmental bodies, such as the Senate subcommittee on Alcoholism and Drug Abuse, the Senate Commerce committee, the Federal Trade Commission, NIAAA, or state legislatures. Investigative hearings should focus on alcohol and ad industry marketing studies, reports, goals and achievements. Television stations and networks should be asked to report on the ratio of alcohol advertisements to public service announcements concerning alcohol, as well as the time of broadcast of public service announcements. Publishers of newspapers and magazines, some of which do not accept alcohol advertising, should testify on any censorship or self-censorship of articles due to alcohol advertising. Hollywood script-writers should describe their efforts to alter the way alcohol is portrayed in movies and on television. The question of "unidentified printed objects," apparent in many alcohol ads, will only be answered when corporate executives testify under oath on the witness stand.

Understandably, the variety of studies and investigations we have suggested will take years. Even if all these studies were done, we believe that no studies will ever demonstrate conclusively the multiple effects that 20 years of exposure to alcohol advertising will have on consumers of various ages and personality types. Considering the massive amount of harm that alcohol is inflicting on our society, we believe it is entirely appropriate and urgent to begin taking common sense actions immediately to alter the marketing of alcoholic beverages.

We are hardly the first to perceive that the marketing of alcoholic beverages should be more tightly controlled. In 1973, the National Commission on Marijuana and Drug Abuse stated:

> Without reviving Prohibition, society can demonstrate to users that alcohol is not an ordinary commodity but, rather, is a powerful psychoactive drug. . . . We further urge manufacturers and distributors of alcoholic beverages to inform the public that compulsive use of alcohol is the most widespread and destructive drug-use pattern in this nation. Advertising should emphasize moderate, responsible use and point out the dangers of excessive consumption. The Commission also recommends that the industry reorient its advertising to avoid making alcohol use attractive to populations especially susceptible to irresponsible use, particularly young people.[114]

An expert committee of the World Health Organization issued a report in 1980 that concluded:

> In view of the potential contribution of well-designed educational and information measures in reducing the demand for alcohol and its untoward consequences, and in preparing for the introduction of control legislation, the Committee recommends that. . . governments should simultaneously undertake a review of their policies with respect to the advertising of alcoholic beverages in order to make them consistent with educational efforts to reduce demand.[115]

We suggest the following steps for reforming alcoholic beverage marketing in the 1980's:

• The Federal Trade Commission or Bureau of Alcohol, Tobacco and Firearms should ban all advertising and marketing efforts aimed at heavy drinkers and young people. This would include activities on college campuses, ads on rock music stations and in youth magazines, commercials on sports broadcasts, and ads that suggest heavy consumption.

• Ads would either be (a) banned from radio and television, or (b) permitted without any limitation, but balanced by an equal number of professionally produced spots highlighting health problems related to alcohol and suggesting alternatives to alcohol.

• The Federal Communications Commission should encourage all broadcasters to run health-oriented and other alcohol-related public service announcements in prime-time, sports, and family-viewing time slots.

• Companies using print advertising should be required to either devote a significant space in each ad to health information or sponsor an equal number of equally well disseminated advertisements containing this information. The FTC or NIAAA could provide sample ads to insure that the public service advertisements are truly in the public interest and not so dull, redundant, or irrelevant that consumers would ignore them after the first few months.

• The content of alcohol advertisements should be limited to consumer information about the taste, price, and composition of products, with no puffery and no association with social, sexual, or financial success. Many retail liquor stores already run austere ads that just list product and price; these ads convey useful consumer information without all the offensive Madison Avenue hype.

• The depiction of risky activities should not be permitted in alcohol advertising.

• Local governments should carefully regulate the time and place of sale of alcoholic beverages. The more outlets selling these beverages, the greater will be alcohol consumption and alcohol problems. Sale at supermarkets, gas stations, and other nontraditional outlets should be halted.

• Sports and other celebrities, active or retired, should not be permitted to appear in ads or otherwise help market alcoholic beverages.

Though we believe that our suggested measures are reasonable in light of the magnitude of America's alcohol problem, they will clearly not be adopted fully or quickly. Furthermore, even if they were adopted completely and immediately, we are not so naive as to argue that these measures alone would have a decisive effect on health problems related to alcohol.

The highly respected British medical journal, *The Lancet*, considered alcohol advertising several years ago and supported a total ban. Based on one study (and not considered definitive), the editors of the journal estimated that a ban on advertising could reduce alcohol consumption by 13 percent. *The Lancet* stated:

> A reduction of consumption by 13 percent may seem modest, but the impact could be considerable. The general view is that a fall in *per capita* consumption is reflected in a greater fall of consumption by heavy drinkers, who of course are those at greatest risk of alcohol-related harm. The likely reduction of consumption in this category has been reckoned as high as 25 percent, so a ban on advertising might save the nation much illness and misery.[116]

Advertising is only one of many forces that influence our drinking habits. Limitations on marketing should not be seen as a panacea, but merely as one element in a comprehensive, coordinated attack on our society's alcohol problem. *The overall goal of this attack should be to change the very way people think about alcohol and drinking.* Drinking can have a place in many of our lives and in our society, but it should never be seen as a way of demonstrating manhood or feminity, of promoting one's chances of success in various endeavors, or of solving personal problems.

Other important corrective measures include:

• massive educational efforts in every community and every classroom in the country;

• warning notices (changing periodically to maintain consumer interest) and calorie contents printed on labels;

• more accurate portrayal in movies and television programming of alcohol's effects;

• expanded employee assistance programs;

• crackdowns on retail outlets that sell to youths or inebriated adults; and

• greater control over the types of products produced and where they are sold and served.

To help pay for these measures, as well as to reimburse society for a fraction of the harm caused by alcohol, federal excise taxes should be raised substantially (they were last raised in 1951 and have been eroded severely by 32 years of inflation). Also, businesses should not be allowed to deduct expenditures for alcohol as a tax-reducing business expense. And costs of alcohol advertising should not be an allowable, tax reducing expense for booze merchants. These tax changes could generate up to about $30 billion in new revenue annually. The tax burden would fall primarily on heavy drinkers, and the revenues should be used, in part, to help treat and prevent the myriad of problems caused by alcohol.

Politicians make sweeping commitments to address alcohol abuse, but direct action is rare. President and Mrs. Reagan have been particularly outspoken in their concern about drinking among children. However, the Reagan Administration has been far more aggressive about "getting government off the backs of business" than about alcohol problems. Thus, it is unlikely that the present administration will take any meaningful action that might reduce alcohol sales.

To pave the way for a more socially concerned future administration, citizens concerned about alcohol's impact on society should establish a blue-ribbon "Citizens Commission on Alcohol Problems," which would develop a wide-ranging, coordinated strategy for individuals, business and industry, non-profits, and government to undertake. Commissioners should include present and former legislators concerned about alcohol, health care experts, religious leaders, former directors of NIAAA, public figures, and philanthropists who have contributed to alcohol programs.

There is one more little-discussed, but vital ingredient for success: human resources. The alcoholic beverage industry has at its beck and call, to lobby, testify, write letters, and give speeches, an army of highly-motivated lawyer-lobbyists, corporate executives, restauranteurs, beer truck drivers, academic consultants, ad agencies, liquor retailers and wholesalers, wine "critics," and media outlets whose profits rely upon alcohol advertising. Who can combat a force like this?

Little progress will be made in reducing the awesome toll alcohol is taking until concerned citizens organize and demand action. Parents of children killed by drunk drivers have recently provided inspiring leadership. But we need more. We need a few brave politicians who will hold tough Congressional hearings. We need brave advertising executives who will disclose information that is well-known to the industry, but kept secret from the public. We need professors who will report on the alcoholic beverage industry without becoming dependent on the industry for grants or psychological support. We need investigative journalists willing to spend months uncovering and describing the *modus operandi* of the $55 billion alcoholic beverage industry. And we need responsible corporate executives within the alcoholic beverage industry. With resources like these, progress is inevitable.

FOOTNOTES

[1]R.E. Berry, J.P. Boland, C.N. Smart, J.R. Kanak, *The Economic Costs of Alcohol Abuse—1975*. Prepared for the National Institute on Alcohol Abuse and Alcoholism, August, 1977.

[2]National Institute on Alcohol Abuse and Alcoholism (NIAAA), *Third Report to Congress*. 1978.

[2a]Office of Technology Assessment, *The Effectiveness and Costs of Alcoholism Treatment*, 1983.

[3]*Impact*, January 15, 1983.

[4]Charles Atkin and Martin Block, *Content and Effect of Alcoholic Beverage Advertising*, Michigan State University, 1980. Prepared for the Bureau of Alcohol, Tobacco and Firearms, Federal Trade Commission, Department of Transportation, and NIAAA.

[5]David J. Pittman, testimony in *Lamar Outdoor Advertising v. Mississippi State Tax Commission*, U.S. Court of Appeals Fifth Circuit, 1982. No. 82-4076.

[6]David J. Pittman and Donald E. Strickland, "A Critical Evaluation of the Control of Consumption Policy," unpublished conference paper, September, 1981. Also Pittman and M. Dow Lambert, "Alcoholism Not Influenced by Media," *Modern Brewery Age*, January, 1979.

[7]Kathleen Ryan, Miller Brewing Company Office of Corporate Affairs, phone interview August 19, 1982.

[8]Sam D. Chilcote, Jr., *Alcohol Health and Research World*, Fall, 1980, p. 43.

[9]Distilled Spirits Council of the United States, *Code of Good Practices*. DISCUS, Washington, D.C.

[10]United States Brewers Association, *Guidelines For Beer Advertising*. USBA, Washington, D.C.

[11]The Wine Institute, *Code of Advertising Standards*. Wine Institute, San Francisco, California.

[12]FTC Memo, September 3, 1981.

[13]FTC Memo, July 30, 1982.

[14]27 Code Fed. Reg. parts 4(G), 5(H), 7(F).

[15]27 U.S.C. 205(f).

[16]Charles C. Sharp, phone interview, August 11, 1982.

[17]*Business Week*, "The King of Beers Still Rules." July 12, 1982.

[18]*The New York Times*, "Budweiser Still No. 1 in Sales." February 16, 1982.

[19]*Marketing and Media Decisions*, "Budweiser's Must Win Attitude," Spring, 1982.

[20]Gavin-Jobson Associates, *The Wine Marketing Handbook, 1979.* New York, N.Y.

[21]Milton Moskowitz, "Grape Expectations," *San Francisco Sunday Examiner and Chronicle*, July 25, 1982.

[22]Gavin-Jobson Associates, *The 1980 Wine Handbook.* New York, N.Y.

[23]*Beverage World 100-Year History 1882-1982* (1982).

[24]*Business Week*, "Creating a Mass Market for Wine." March 15, 1982.

[25]*Advertising Age*, March 29, 1982.

[26]*Impact*, "Distilled Spirits Market Review and Forecast 1981," Shanken Communications, New York, N.Y.

[27]*Advertising Age*, January 31, 1983.

[28]*Advertising Age*, August 16, 1982.

[29]*Impact*, "Distilled Spirts Market Review and Forecast 1980," Shanken Communications, New York, N.Y.

[30]Charles G. Burck, "The Whiskey Distillers Put Up Their Dukes," *Fortune*, September, 1977.

[31]*Advertising Age*, June 14, 1982.

[32]Vincent Machi, Ninth Annual Conference, Distilled Spirits Council of the U.S., January 25, 1982.

[33]Meyer Katzper, Ralph Rayback, Marc Hertzman, "Alcohol Beverage Advertisement and Consumption," *Journal of Drug Issues*, Fall, 1978.

[34]NIAAA, "Fact Sheet: Estimated Patterns of American Adult Drinking Habits." National Clearinghouse for Alcohol Information, Rockville, Maryland. Feburary, 1981.

[35]*Alcoholism/The National Magazine*, Jan.-Feb., 1983.

[36]Richard B. Herzog, testimony before the Senate Subcommittee on Alcoholism and Narcotics. March 11, 1976.

[37]Russell L. Ackoff and James R. Emshoff, "Advertising Research at Anheuser-Busch, Inc. (1968-1974)," *Sloan Management Review*, Spring, 1975.

[38]Marc Hertzman, testimony in *Lamar v. Mississippi State Tax Commission*, U.S. Court of Appeals Fifth Circuit, 1982. No. 82-4076.

[39]*Business Week*, July 12, 1982.

[40]*Advertising Age*, June 25, 1982.

[41]*Los Angeles Times*, August 24, 1982

[42]Robert E. McDowell, "How We Did It—Beer's Main Title Bout: It's Miller vs. Budweiser," *Marketing Times*. November-December, 1981.

[43]*Berkeley Gazette*, "Busch Finds Simple Equation Sells Beer," April 26, 1982.

[44]*Beverage World*, "Selling More Beer With Sports Promotion," July, 1981.

[45]*Advertising Age*, May 31, 1982.

[46]Warren Breed and James R. DeFoe, "Risk and Alcohol Lifestyle Advertising," *Abstracts and Reviews in Alcohol and Driving*. September, 1981.

[47]*Advertising Age*, August 2, 1982.

[48]National Institute on Drug Abuse, *Student Drug Use in America, 1975-1981*. (1982).

[49]NIAAA, "The Public Health Approach to Problems Associated with Alcohol Consumption," chart I-11, 1980.

[50]Atkin and Block, *op. cit.*, pp. 195, 197.

[51]*The Wall Street Journal*, February 8, 1983. Also see *The New York Times*, August 22, 1982.

[52]American Insurance Association, "Digest of State Laws Relating to Drinking Under the Influence of Alcohol." (1982).

[53]James R. DeFoe and Warren Breed, "The Problem of Alcohol Advertisements in College Newspapers," *The Journal of American College Health Associations*, February, 1979.

[54]Nicholas Johnson, testimony before the Senate Subcommittee on Alcoholism and Narcotics, Committee on Labor and Public Welfare, March 1976. The hearings were held on alcohol advertising.

[55]Atkins and Block, *op. cit*, p. 15.

[56]Robert L. Hammond, testimony before the Senate Subcommittee on Alcoholism and Narcotics, March 11, 1976.

[57]CASS Student Advertising Inc., *Campus Monitor Series*, Spring, 1982. Evanston, Illinois.

[58]Telephone interview, February 24, 1983.

[59]Alan Weston Communications, Research department, telephone interview, August 31, 1982.

[60]Steven Walfish, D. Stenmark, D. Wentz, C. Myers, D.Linares, *Intern. J. or Addictions, 16*: 941-5 (1981).

[61]CASS Student Advertising, Inc., *1981-82 National Rate Book and College Newspaper Directory*. Evanston, Illinois.

[62]"Rates and Data, 1983," *Newsweek*.

[63]Barbara Kane, *National Lampoon* Advertising department, telephone interview, August 19, 1982.

[64]*Ms.*, Advertising department, August 20, 1982.

[65]Bob Seaver, DISCUS, telephone interview. August 16, 1982.

[66]Marvin Gropp, Director of Research for the Magazine Advertising Bureau, New York, N.Y., telephone interview, August 20, 1982. A recent study by the Bureau showed the percentage of magazine ads by quarter: First, 21.0; Second, 26.5; Third, 21.5; Fourth, 31.0.

[67]*Advertising Age*, February 23, 1981.

[68]*Spring Break: A Playboy Annual*, March 1982. Published by College Marketing and Research Corporation, Playboy Enterprises, New York, N.Y.

[69]*Advertising Age*, April 26, 1982.

[70]Geraldo M. Gonzalez, "Alcohol Use and Level of Knowledge About Alcohol Among Students Who Visited Daytona Beach, Florida During Their Spring Break 1981," unpublished. Sponsored by BACCHUS, a college-based educational organization for the prevention of alcohol abuse. Gonzalez is the president as well as the Director of Campus Alcohol Information Center, University of Florida.

[71]Telephone interview, February 18, 1983.

[72]*Advertising Age*, July 26, 1982.

[73]Nassau Coliseum, Public Relations office, August 18, 1982.

[74]Don Kirshner Entertainment Corporation, New York, N.Y., August 18, 1982.

[75]Warner Brothers Records, Publicity, Burbank, California, August 18, 1982.

[76]Telephone interview, March 3, 1983.

[77]Atkin and Block, *op cit.*, p. 53.

[78]John Quick, manager of ratings for CBS Television, telephone interview, August 11, 1982.

[79]Tim Brooks,NBC Television Research, telephone interview, August 11, 1982.

[80]National Institute of Mental Health, "Television and Behavior," (1982).

[81]Atkin and Block, *op. cit.*, p. 306.

[82]Atkin and Block, *op. cit.*, p. 31.

[83]Gavin-Jobson Associates, *The 1980 Liquor Handbook.*

[84]Elliot Wendt, "Can Sex Sell Light Beer?," *Beverage World*, September, 1981.

[85]*The New York Times*, June 9, 1981.

[86]*The New York Times*, December 22, 1981.

[87]*The Washington Post*, December 22, 1982.

[88]*The New York Times*, August 10, 1982.

[89]*Fortune* October, 1976.

[90]Bill Abrams, "Selling Wine Like Soda Pop, Riunite Uncorks Huge Market," *The Wall Street Journal*, July 2, 1981.

[91]*The Washington Post*, December 22, 1982.

[92]*Advertising Age*, February 15, 1982.

[93]*Advertising Age*, August 31, 1981.

[94]Tom Horton, "How About a Six-pack of Chablis?," *Express*, September, 1981. *Express* is Amtrack's complimentary travel magazine.

[95]*Advertising Age*, September 20, 1982.

[96]*Advertising Age*, July 27, 1981.

[97]*Wine and Spirit*, October, 1980.

[98]*J. Psychedelic Drugs 12*: 1 (1980).

[99]*Advertising Age*, August 7, 1978.

[100]Charles Sharp, testimony before the Senate Committee on Commerce, Science and Transportation, May 10, 1982. Hearings were held on health warning labels for cigarettes.

[101]Atkin and Block, *op. cit.*, pp. 284-85.

[102]Atkin and Block, *op. cit.*, p. 20.

[103]Warren Breed and James R. DeFoe, "Themes in Magazine Alcohol Advertisements: A Critique," *Journal of Drug Issues*, Fall, 1979.

[104]Atkin and Block, *op. cit.*, pp. 332-34.

[105]Atkin and Block, *op. cit.*, p. 30.

[106]27 Code Fed. Reg. 5.65.

[107]Key, Wilson Bryan, *Subliminal Seduction*, Signet (New York), 1974.

[108]Notice of Proposed Rulemaking, 45 *Federal Register* 83530, December 12, 1980.

[109]Telephone call, February 15, 1983.

[110]Joy Moser, *Prevention of Alcohol-Related Problems*, World Health Organization and Alcoholism and Drug Addiction Research Foundation, 1980.

[111]Liquor License Board of Ontario, *Directives on Advertising and Sales Promotions for Beer, Wine and Cider Industries, October, 1980.*

[112]*Channels, June-July, 1982, p. 8.*

[113]*Advertising Age*, January 10, 1983, p. M-22.

[114]National Commission on Marihuana and Drug Abuse, *Second Report*, March, 1973.

[115]WHO Expert Committee, *Problems Related to Alcohol Consumption*, Tech. Report Series 650, 1980.

[116]*The Lancet* , p. 1175 (November 29, 1980).

APPENDIX

1. Alcoholic Beverage Producers Among The Top 100 Leading National Advertisers

Company	Rank	1982 Ad Budget
Alcohol Producer		
Anheuser-Busch	22	$243.4 million
Seagram	44	153.0
Brown-Forman Distillers	76	74.0
Stroh Brewing Co.	90	55.5
Hiram Walker Resources	98	44.4
E&J Gallo Winery	99	42.9
Conglomerates & Alcohol Subsidiaries		
R. J. Reynolds	4	$530.3 million
Heublein, Inc.		
Philip Morris:	5	$501.7
Miller Brewing Company		
Norton Simon Inc.	33	
Somerset Importers		$191.2
American Brands:	78	
Jim B. Beam Distilling		$72.3

Source: **Advertising Age,** September 8, 1983

2. Alcoholic Beverage Producers Among Top 25 Advertisers By Medium

Newspaper
  Seagram – 23rd

Magazine:
  Seagram – 5th
  Hiram Walker – 24th

Network Radio:
  Anheuser-Busch – 13th

Spot Radio:
  Anheuser-Busch – 1st
  Stroh – 10th
  Adolph Coors Brewing – 16th
  Van Munching – 21st

Network TV
  Anheuser-Busch – 11th

Outdoor:
  Seagram – 5th
  National Distillers – 9th
  Hiram Walker – 7th
  Brown-Forman – 8th
  Anheuser-Busch – 11th
  Bacardi – 22nd
  G. Heileman Brewing Co. – 23rd

Source: **Advertising Age,** September 8, 1983

3. Top Ten Beer Advertisers (1982)*

Anheuser-Busch	$193.9 million
Miller (Philip Morris)	137.9
Stroh	45.5
Coors	32.2
G. Heileman	21.9
Van Munching	21.9
Olympia	16.7
Pabst	14.3
Martlet Importing	11.0
Genessee	6.2

*Source: **Impact**, September, 1983. These figures do not include non-advertising forms of marketing, such as discount coupons, free beer parties, signs for taverns, T-shirt sales, etc.

4. Who Owns Whom in the Alcohol World?

Coca-Cola (N.Y.)	owns	Franzia Wines
Seagram	owns	Christian Brothers; Paul Masson wines; Wine Spectrum (Taylor California Cellars)
Heublein (see RJR below)	owns	United Vintners (Inglenook wine)
National Distillers	owns	Almadén wines
Norton-Simon (Avis, Hunt-Wesson, Max Factor, etc.)	owns	Somerset Importers (Johnnie Walker scotch, Tanqueray gin)
Philip Morris (cigarettes)	owns	Miller beer
Liggett (L&M cigarettes)	owns	J&B scotch, Grand Marnier liqueur, Bailey's Original Irish Cream, Bombay gin, Absolut vodka, Piat d'Or wine
R.J. Reynolds Industries (Winston and Camel cigarettes, Chun King and Del Monte foods)	owns	Heublein (Black Velvet whiskey, Smirnoff vodka, Harvey's Bristol Cream sherry, Lancer's wine, Jose Cuervo tequila)
American Brands (Pall Mall, Carlton, Lucky Strike cigarettes; Sunshine biscuits; Master locks)	owns	Jim Beam whiskey
Stroh	owns	Schlitz; Schaeffer

STATEMENT ON ALCOHOL BEVERAGE ADVERTISING

Alcohol abuse and alcoholism cause a massive amount of harm to millions of Americans, to our economy, and to our social fabric. Cirrhosis of the liver, traffic fatalities, broken careers, birth defects, spouse-beating: these and other alcohol-related misfortunes constitute a virtual epidemic in our society. The massive amount of advertising for alcoholic beverages can only increase alcohol consumption and the inevitable consequences.

Despite the apparent ubiquity of alcohol advertising, since the end of Prohibition, the liquor and broadcasting industries have supported one important, voluntary limitation that has been of inestimable benefit to the public: liquor advertisements have not been broadcast on radio and television. This socially responsible restriction has been reinforced by advertising codes of the major broadcasting and distilled spirits trade associations. Though the broadcasters' code has been suspended recently, virtually all radio and television stations continue to respect the ban on liquor ads.

The absence of liquor advertising on radio and television is most welcome. We urge the liquor and broadcasting industries to maintain this practice. Furthermore, we believe that the marketing approaches that are currently being used on an unprecedented scale to sell alcoholic beverages should be reexamined in light of the enormous harm that we know alcohol is causing in our society, to drinkers and non-drinkers alike. *As a first step, we urge that the voluntary ban on broadcast liquor advertising be extended to beer and wine.*

William Hathaway
Former Senator from Maine

Nicholas Johnson
Former commissioner of the Federal
Communications Commission

John R. DeLuca
Former director of National Institute
on Alcohol Abuse and Alcoholism

Dr. Ernest Noble
Former director of National Institute
on Alcohol Abuse and Alcoholism

—*October, 1982*

Calling the Shots is an excellent film on alcoholic beverage advertising. The film features Jean Kilbourne, who has studied and lectured on the subject of advertising for years. The film includes numerous examples of ads that carry subtle psychological meanings and is chock full of facts and figures about the impact of alcohol advertising. *Calling the Shots* is ideal for stimulating discussion in high school and college classes or community groups.

The film is available for rental or purchase in 16mm or ¾-inch videocassette formats. It is accompanied by a brochure of Alcohol Awareness Resources compiled by Dr. Kilbourne. For more information, contact: *Cambridge Documentary Films, P.O. Box 385, Cambridge, Massachusetts, 02139 or call (617) 354-3677.*

Authors' Biographies

Michael Jacobson, executive director of the Center for Science in the Public Interest, holds a Ph.D. in microbiology from the Massachusetts Institute of Technology. He is the author of *Eater's Digest, Nutrition Scoreboard,* and co-author of *Food for People, Not for Profit* as well as writing numerous articles and booklets on nutrition and health. He also served as editor of the CSPI book *Chemical Additives in Booze* released last year.

Robert Atkins, a former researcher for CSPI, holds a B.A. from Columbia University. He is now working as an aide to Congressman Robert Torricelli (D-N.J.).

George Hacker, associate director of alcohol policies for CSPI, received a law degree from the University of Denver. He has worked with CSPI in organizing the National Alcohol Tax Coalition and Citizens Concerned About Alcohol Advertising.

INDEX